W9-BMY-594

Level A

READ FOR REAL

Nonfiction Strategies for Reading Results

Authors

Leslie W. Crawford, Ed.D.
Professor of Literacy
Georgia College & State University

Charles E. Martin, Ph.D.
Professor of Early Childhood and Middle Grades Education
Georgia College & State University

Margaret M. Philbin, Ed.D.
Associate Professor Emerita
State University of New York Potsdam

Vocabulary and Fluency Consultant

Timothy V. Rasinski, Ph.D.
Professor of Education
Kent State University

English Language Learner Specialist

Caroline Teresa Linse, Ed.D.
Fulbright Scholar
Minsk State Linguistic University
Minsk, Belarus

Zaner-Bloser

Photo Credits

Cover: (woman firefighter) Jim Zuckerman/CORBIS; (chimp) Tom Brakefield/CORBIS; (acrobat) Rune Hellestad/CORBIS; (Cousteau) Bettmann/CORBIS; (lightning) Larry Lee/CORBIS; (L. Armstrong) Pascal Pavanni/AFP/Getty.

Models: George C. Anderson Photography

pp. 3, 47, 48, 58(R), 60, 62, 64, 71(B), Kennan Ward/CORBIS; pp. 4, 117(R), 140(L), 140(R), 141(I), 144, Courtesy of NASA; pp. 5, 152, 155, Courtesy of NOAA; pp. 8, 11, Robert Maass/CORBIS; pp. 9(L), 23, TOUHIG SION/CORBIS SYGMA; pp. 9(R), 33, Zaner-Bloser, Inc.; pp. 10(L), 14(T), 44, Jim Zuckerman/CORBIS; pp. 10(R), 12, J. Barry O'Rourke/CORBIS; p. 13, First Light/CORBIS; p. 14(B), William A. Bake/CORBIS; p. 15, George Shelley/CORBIS; pp. 22(L), 28, Dan Guravich/CORBIS; pp. 22(R), 24, 34, Tom Stewart/CORBIS; p. 25, Jeffery Allan Salter/CORBIS SABA; pp. 27, 89, 157, 189(L), 190(L), 190(R), 193, 194, 196(I), 208, Reuters/CORBIS; pp. 32(L), 36, 116, 118(L), 119, 122, 143, CORBIS; pp. 32(R), 35(T), Ronnie Kaufman/CORBIS; p. 35(B), Paul Barton/CORBIS; pp. 45(L), 59, Renee Lynn/CORBIS; pp. 45(R), 69, Staffan Widstrand/CORBIS; pp. 46(L), 52, William Manning/CORBIS; pp. 46(R), 49, Ralph A. Clevenger/CORBIS; p. 51, Gallo Images/CORBIS; pp. 58(L), 63, Tom Brakefield/CORBIS; pp. 68(L), 73(T), Stuart Westmorland/CORBIS; pp. 68(R), 71(T), 72, Brandon D. Cole/CORBIS; p. 73(B), Vince Streano/CORBIS; pp. 80, 83, STEFF/CORBIS KIPA; pp. 81(L), 95, Paul A. Souders/CORBIS; pp. 81(R), 104(L), 104(R), 105, 106, 108, 109(B), 154(L), 160, Joseph Sohm; ChromoSohm Inc./CORBIS; pp. 82(L), 85, Rune Hellestad/CORBIS; pp. 82(R), 84, CORBIS SYGMA; p. 86, Rune Hellestad/CORBIS/SYGMA; pp. 94(L), 99, Michael DeYoung/CORBIS; pp. 94(R), 96(B), 98(T), Douglas Peebles/CORBIS; p. 96(T), Jay Dickman/CORBIS; p. 97, Mike Powell/Getty Images; p. 107(B), Tom & Dee Ann McCarthy/CORBIS; pp. 117(L), 123, 130(L), 131, 134(B), 154(R), 159(B), 168, 189(R), 203, 204(B), 212(L), 213, 217(T), Bettmann/CORBIS; pp. 118(R), 121, James Randklev; Visions of America/CORBIS; p. 120, Graham White; pp. 130(R), 133, Jeffrey L. Rotman/CORBIS; p. 136, Forestier Yves/CORBIS SYGMA; p. 141, NASA/Roger Ressmeyer/CORBIS; p. 142, Matthew Mcvay/CORBIS; p. 145(B), AFP/GETTY; pp. 153(L), 167, A & J Verkaik/CORBIS; pp. 153(R), 177, James A. Sugar/CORBIS; p. 158, Steve Starr/CORBIS; p. 159(T), Philip Wallick/CORBIS; pp. 166(L), 170, Larry Lee/CORBIS; pp. 166(R), 169(T), Tom Ives/CORBIS; p. 169(B), Jeff Vanuga/CORBIS; pp. 176(L), 178, Dave G. Houser/CORBIS; pp. 176(R), 180(B), Hans Georg Roth/CORBIS; p. 180(T), Digital image © 1996 CORBIS; Original image courtesy of NASA/CORBIS; pp. 188, 191, Pascal Pavanni/AFP/Getty; p. 192, Patrick Kovarik/AFP/Getty; p. 196, Tim De Waele/Isosport/CORBIS; pp. 202(L), 206, David Madison/NewSport/CORBIS; pp. 202(R), 204(T), Karl Weatherly/CORBIS; p. 205, Tony Duffy/Getty; pp. 212(R), 215, Tom Hauck/Getty; p. 216, J.D. Cuban/Getty.

Art Credits

pp. 16, 26, 37, 50, 61, 70, 87, 98(B), 107(T), 109(B), 124, 134(T), 135, 145(T), 156, 172, 179, 195, 207, 217(B), Inkwell Publishing Solutions, Inc.

Editorial, production, and photo research by Inkwell Publishing Solutions, Inc.

ISBN 0-7367-2351-X

Copyright © 2005 Zaner-Bloser, Inc.

All rights reserved. No part of this book may be reproduced or transmitted in any form or by any means, electronic or mechanical, including photocopying, recording, or by any information storage and retrieval system, without permission in writing from the Publisher. The Publisher has made every effort to trace the ownership of all copyrighted material and to secure the necessary permissions to reprint these selections. In the event of any question arising as to the use of any material, the Publisher, while expressing regret for any inadvertent error, will be happy to make any necessary corrections.

Zaner-Bloser, Inc., P.O. Box 16764, Columbus, Ohio 43216-6764 (1-800-421-3018)

Printed in the United States of America

07 08 09 10 (330) 9 8 7 6 5

Table of Contents

Table of Contents (continued)

Hi! We're your
READ FOR REAL
Reading Team Partners!

Have you noticed that the reading you do in science and social studies is different from reading stories and novels? Reading nonfiction <u>is</u> different. When you read nonfiction, you learn new information. We'll introduce you to some strategies that will help you read and understand nonfiction.

In each unit, you'll learn three strategies—one to use **Before** you read, one to use **During** your reading, and one to use **After** you read. You'll work with these strategies in all three reading selections in each unit.

In the first selection, you'll **Learn** the unit strategies. When you see a red button like this ◉, read "My Thinking" notes to see how one of us used the strategy.

In the second selection in each unit, you'll **Practice** the strategies by jotting down your own notes about how you used the same unit strategies. The red button ◉ will tell you where to stop and think about the strategies.

When you read the last selection in each unit, you'll **Apply** the strategies. You'll decide when to stop and take notes as you read.

Strategies

Here they are—the **Before, During, and After** Reading Strategies.

Use these strategies with all your nonfiction reading—social studies and science textbooks, magazine and newspaper articles, Web sites, and more.

	BEFORE READING	DURING READING	AFTER READING
UNIT 1	**Preview the Selection** by looking at the title and headings to predict what the selection will be about.	**Make Connections** by relating information that I already know about the subject to what I'm reading.	**Recall** by summarizing the selection in writing or out loud.
UNIT 2	**Activate Prior Knowledge** by looking at the title, headings, pictures, and graphics to decide what I know about this topic.	**Interact With Text** by identifying the main idea and supporting details.	**Evaluate** by searching the selection to determine how the author used evidence to reach conclusions.
UNIT 3	**Set a Purpose** by using the title and headings to write questions that I can answer while I am reading.	**Clarify Understanding** by using photographs, charts, and other graphics to help me understand what I'm reading.	**Respond** by drawing logical conclusions about the topic.
UNIT 4	**Preview the Selection** by looking at the photographs, illustrations, captions, and graphics to predict what the selection will be about.	**Make Connections** by comparing my experiences with what I'm reading.	**Recall** by using the headings to question myself about what I read.
UNIT 5	**Activate Prior Knowledge** by reading the introduction and/or summary to decide what I know about this topic.	**Interact With Text** by identifying how the text is organized.	**Evaluate** by forming a judgment about whether the selection was objective or biased.
UNIT 6	**Set a Purpose** by skimming the selection to decide what I want to know about this subject.	**Clarify Understanding** by deciding whether the information I'm reading is fact or opinion.	**Respond** by forming my own opinion about what I've read.

Now that you've met the team, it's time to get started.

Unit 1

Strategies

Preview the Selection

by looking at the title and headings to predict what the selection will be about.

Make Connections

by relating information that I already know about the subject to what I'm reading.

Recall

by summarizing the selection in writing or out loud.

LEARN
the **strategies**
in the selection
Firefighters
page 11

PRACTICE
the strategies
in the selection
Veterinarians
page 23

APPLY
the strategies
in the selection
Social Workers
page 33

Think About the Strategies

BEFORE READING

Preview the Selection
by looking at the title and headings to predict what the selection will be about.

My Thinking
The strategy says to look at the titles and headings to predict what the selection will be about. This means I'll try to figure out what is going to happen next. The title is "Firefighters" The headings all refer to something about firefighters. I predict that this selection will be about firefighters. Maybe I'll learn how they put out fires. Maybe I'll learn how to become a firefighter. Now I'm ready to read and see if I'm right.

DURING READING

Make Connections
by relating information that I already know about the subject to what I'm reading.

My Thinking
This strategy says to make connections by relating information that I already know about the subject to what I am reading. I will stop and think about this strategy every time I come to a red button like this ●.

Firefighters

Firefighters take the quick route to the fire truck.

A **siren** goes off in the firehouse. A nearby building is in **flames**. People may be trapped on the top floor.

Six firefighters have been eating dinner. At the sound of the alarm, the firefighters react. They push away from the table. They leave their meal. Down the pole they slide. Quickly, they put on their special pants, coats, boots, and helmets with hoods. They jump on the fire truck.

On Their Way to a Fire

On their way out of the station, the driver—called a **chauffeur**—grabs a paper from a computer. It gives the

Vo·cab·u·lar·y

siren (**sy**•ruhn)—something that makes a loud sound

flames—heat and light given off by a fire

chauffeur (**shoh**•fuhr)— a person who is hired to drive

Strategy

Make Connections by relating information that I already know about the subject to what I'm reading.

My Thinking

I know that fire-fighters put out fires, but I never thought about what firefighters talk about on the way to a fire.

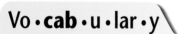

Vo·cab·u·lar·y

revolve (ri•volv)—to turn around repeatedly in a circle

respond (ri•spond)—to react

emergency (i•mur•juhn•see) —a risky situation that must be dealt with fast

scene (seen)—the place where something happens

rescue (res•kyoo)— the saving of someone who is in danger

address of the place that is on fire. The driver gets other information, too. The paper tells how many floors the building has. Time is short. Fires move fast and so must the firefighters.

Within seconds, the truck blasts from the station. The siren screams. Lights **revolve** and flash. People on the street must get out of the way. Cars should keep back. They should let the firefighters through to do their job. When a car gets too close, a loud horn warns it to keep away.

The firefighters know just what to do. After all, they've been trained in how to **respond**. Still, this is a dangerous job. Fires are always a real **emergency**.

Firefighters want to make it to the **scene** as fast as they can. Their job is to **rescue** people and pets. They also rescue property. And, they must protect themselves and other firefighters from getting hurt.

No time can be wasted as the firefighters race to a fire.

On the way to the blaze, firefighters talk. How many people are in danger? How close are the fire hydrants to the building? Will the wind fan the fire? Are other buildings on fire, too? At times, firefighters don't really call it "the fire." They give it another name like "the beast." That's because a fire is like a monster. They want to tame this monster.

Like other people, firefighters have feelings. New fire-fighters—called rookies—feel nervous. Rescuing people is risky work. Hearts pound as the crew nears the scene.

Pulses race. But they approach the burning building with a plan. Each firefighter knows his or her job. They must be brave. They must show courage as they face the beast.

Firefighters are brave and courageous people. But they also must be prepared. They have to know how to do their jobs. They must have training.

Training

Imagine going to a school where you wear an air tank on your back. Then think of yourself climbing a four-story ladder. Now picture yourself in a smoky house. You are crawling on the floor. Those are some of the things a trainee does at a Fire Academy.

Firefighters practice on a burn building.

At this school, trainees learn how to use special **gear** and **equipment**. They also study how fires spread. Most important, they practice putting out fires in a "burn building." A burn building is a place where the fire department starts fires. There, the trainees practice how to enter the place. They practice putting out the flames. They do this over and over again.

At the end of six weeks, they must pass the tests. Not everyone **graduates**. Some don't like wearing a breathing mask. Others have trouble climbing high. A few can't work on a team. They might not be strong enough.

Those who graduate know how to fight fires. They're ready for their first real fire call.

Strategy

Make Connections by relating information that I already know about the subject to what I'm reading.

My Thinking
I know that firefighters get training in what to do. But I didn't know there's a special "burn building" where they practice.

Vo·cab·u·lar·y

gear (geer)—equipment or clothing

equipment (i•**kwip**•muhnt)—the tools and machines needed to do something

graduates (**graj**•oo•ayts)—completes a course of study in school and gets a diploma

Special Gear

Firefighters never go near a fire **unprepared**. They have special things to keep them safe. Next time you see firefighters on the job, look for all of the special gear they must wear.

Firefighters must wear a special coat. With this coat, the firefighter's skin is safe from heat and water. The bands glow in the dark. Firefighters can easily be seen.

Firefighters also wear special pants. How many **layers** do these pants have? If you said three, you'd be right! These special pants protect the firefighter's legs. The pants are heavy. Firefighters use suspenders to hold them up! Some suspenders are red. Others are blue.

Every part of the firefighter must be covered. This includes their head. They have a special helmet with earflaps. This gear protects the face, hair, ears, and neck.

Firefighters are prepared.

Firefighters have special coats, pants, helmets, and boots.

Vo·**cab**·u·lar·y

unprepared (un•pri•**paird**)— not ready

layers (**lay**•uhrz)—thicknesses of something

What do you think is special about a firefighter's boots? These boots have steel inside. They stop sharp things from hurting the firefighter's feet.

Air tanks help firefighters breathe. Breathing smoke can be deadly. The air tank has enough good air for 30 minutes. When the air runs low, a whistle sounds. It warns the firefighter to leave the building.

Firefighters must be fit. They must be strong enough to lift heavy things. Years ago, the air tank might have weighed 20 pounds. Today, the tank is lighter, but hardly light!

Firefighters must stay safe so they can help those in need. The special gear they must wear is important—it keeps them safe!

The Mascot

Firefighters help others. But a fire dog helps firefighters. No, the dog doesn't hold the water hose. The dog is a **mascot** who brings good luck. Why Dalmatians? Long ago, this breed **guarded** the firefighters' horses. Today, they make firefighters feel good by riding in the truck.

Strategy

Make Connections by relating information that I already know about the subject to what I'm reading.

My Thinking
I've seen pictures of Dalmatians with firefighters. Now I know that the two have a long history of being together.

Dalmatians are loved and valued by the fire crew.

Vo·cab·u·lar·y

mascot (mas•kot)—someone or something believed to bring good luck

guarded (gard•id)—protected

The Rescue

When a truck races to a fire, many things happen at once. The engine company puts out the fire. The ladder company lets the smoke escape. In a rescue, the firefighters search the building. When they return to the firehouse, someone writes a report. The **crew** is tired. But they know they have done a good job.

So why do these brave men and women want to do such a dangerous job? As one firefighter says, "I just want to help people. I can't imagine doing anything else!"

Firefighters are called heroes. Every day, they risk their lives to keep us safe.

Keep It Safe

How can you keep your house free of fires? Do not play with matches. You don't want a flame to jump to other things. Careless cigarette smoking is the leading cause of home fire deaths. Also, tell your family to be careful in the kitchen. Don't let the stove flame touch other things that burn, such as paper. As you can see in the chart below, most house fires start in the kitchen.

What percentage of fires start in the kitchen?

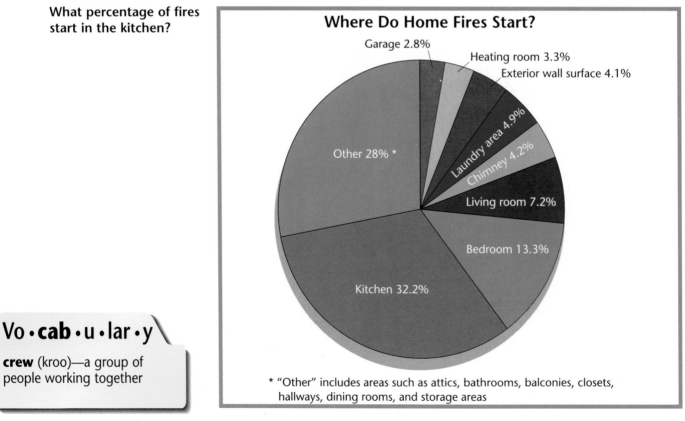

Where Do Home Fires Start?

- Garage 2.8%
- Heating room 3.3%
- Exterior wall surface 4.1%
- Laundry area 4.9%
- Chimney 4.2%
- Living room 7.2%
- Bedroom 13.3%
- Kitchen 32.2%
- Other 28% *

* "Other" includes areas such as attics, bathrooms, balconies, closets, hallways, dining rooms, and storage areas

Vo·**cab**·u·lar·y

crew (kroo)—a group of people working together

Talk to your parents today. Ask them to check your smoke alarm. Make sure it works. If a fire starts, the alarm's noise will tell you there's a problem. Together, your family can decide what to do next.

Make sure you have an emergency plan. Decide on a family meeting place. Make sure every family member knows it. This way, family members and firefighters will know everyone is safe. Hopefully, you will never have to use the plan. But, just in case, make sure everyone in the family knows what to do in case of a fire.

Think About the Strategy

AFTER READING

Recall

by summarizing the selection in writing or out loud.

My Thinking

The strategy says to summarize the selection in writing or out loud. I can do that by writing or telling about the main parts of the selection. I learned that firefighters have to move fast when the alarm sounds. They must make it to the fire to rescue people and pets. On their way to the fire, they talk about what they are going to do.

Firefighters must go through a lot of training before they are ready to put out real fires. They have a lot of special gear to help them keep safe. They even have mascots, Dalmatians, to bring them luck.

It is our job to make sure our houses are safe and that we know what to do in case of fire.

Graphic organizers help us organize the information we read. I think this text can be organized by using a spider map. Here is how I organized the information. I put the main ideas on each leg of the spider. Then I put details about the main ideas on the lines coming from the legs.

Spider Map

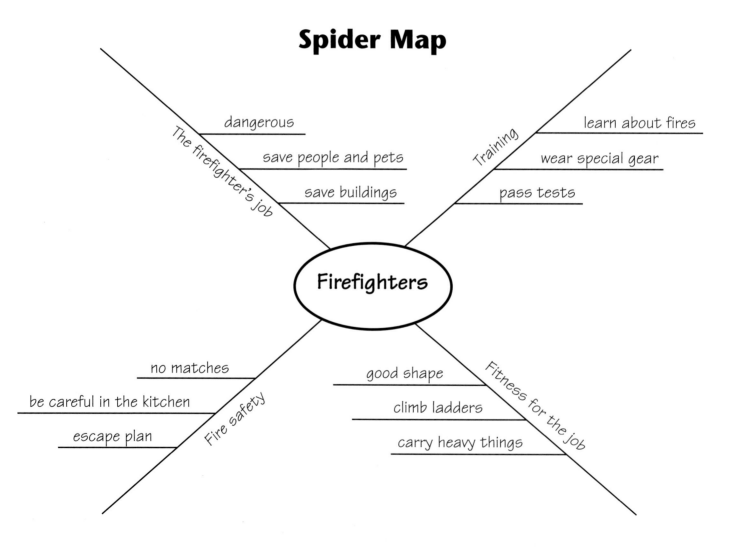

The firefighter's job
- dangerous
- save people and pets
- save buildings

Training
- learn about fires
- wear special gear
- pass tests

Fire safety
- no matches
- be careful in the kitchen
- escape plan

Fitness for the job
- good shape
- climb ladders
- carry heavy things

Firefighters

I used my graphic organizer to write a summary of the article. Can you find the information in my summary that came from my spider map?

A Summary of
Firefighters

Firefighters have an important job. They must have special training and stay in shape. They must be ready because they save lives.

Firefighters have a dangerous job. They stop houses and other buildings from burning. They also save people's lives. They save pets, and they try to save the buildings, too.

At school, trainees learn how fires start and how they spread. They learn how to put out fires. They must practice every day. They wear special clothes and use equipment that protects them from flames and smoke. Hats, pants, and coats protect them from flames. Masks protect them from smoke. After six weeks, the trainees must pass tests. Graduates know how to fight fires. As graduated firefighters, they are prepared to fight a real fire.

Firefighters must be in good shape. They climb tall ladders and crawl on the floor. They have to lift and carry heavy things.

Parents and children can work together at home to decide how to prevent fires. A good rule is not to play with matches. Always be careful at home, especially in the kitchen. Families should make an escape plan in case of a fire.

Firefighters are heroes. They risk their lives every day to help others. They are very brave.

Introduction
My introductory paragraph tells readers what they are about to read.

Body
Each paragraph has information from one leg of my spider map. The first paragraph tells about a firefighter's job. The second paragraph is about the training they go through. I wrote about fitness in the third paragraph. And the fourth body paragraph is about fire safety.

Conclusion
I concluded my paper by recalling the main idea.

Prefixes

Sometimes a word part can give you a clue about a word's meaning. A **prefix** is a word part at the beginning of a word. A prefix can change the meaning of the word.

The prefix *re-* means "again, back, or after." Here are examples from "Firefighters" that have a word with the prefix *re-*.

At the sound of the alarm, the firefighters **react**.
React means "to respond to something that has happened."

Lights **revolve** *and flash*.
Revolve means "to go around again."

After all, they've been trained in how to **respond**.
Respond means "to answer back."

Here are other words with the prefix *re-*.

Theresa had to *revise* her homework.
Revise means "to do again."

Jason will *realign* the papers if the wind blows them away again.
Realign means "to straighten again or align again."

"I want to *revamp* my kitchen and get all new things," said Judy.
Revamp means "to restore."

The reporter will *review* her story before turning it in.
Review means "to go over again."

Francis had to *retrace* her steps to find the bracelet that slipped off her wrist.
Retrace means "to go back over something."

Read these sentences. On a separate sheet of paper, write the meaning of each boldface word. Use what you know about the prefix *re-* to help you.

1. José **reread** the paragraph that he didn't understand.
2. The medicine **restored** the patient to health.
3. Jennifer **reused** the stack of paper.
4. Jonathan **returned** the sweater that did not fit.
5. The drums signaled the troops to **retreat**.

Readers' Theater

Practice reading this script aloud with three other students until you can read it with expression. When you are ready, read it to your classmates.

TIP

As you practice reading this script, show the excitement in your voice that the characters would be feeling.

Narrator: A siren goes off in the firehouse. The firefighters leave their meal. Down the pole they slide. They quickly put on their special gear.

Chief Egan: Let's go!

Chauffeur Kelly: Is everybody in place?

Narrator: They are, so Chauffeur Kelly climbs into the driver's seat of the fire truck. She starts the revolving lights and the siren. The truck roars out.

Egan: Here's what we know. It's a three-story house at the northeast corner of Main and Beverly. Smoke is coming out of the third floor. A fire hydrant is just a few houses away from the scene.

Firefighter Jim: How many people inside?

Kelly: Two.

Jim: Any other buildings involved?

Kelly: No.

Jim: You want me up the ladder?

Egan: Yes, you and Pat. Kelly and I will go in through the front and back doors.

Narrator: The truck arrives at the house.

Kelly: I see smoke but no flames.

Egan: Everybody out! Be careful!

Narrator: The firefighters file out of the truck. Egan and Kelly see that all people and pets have left the building. Jim and Pat climb the ladder and chop at the roof with their axes. Smoke billows out. Other firefighters direct water onto the house. Soon the chief comes outside.

Egan: A grease fire started in the kitchen. It's out now. It's under control.

Narrator: The firefighters stay for two hours to make sure things are fine. Once again, they have risked their lives to keep people safe. They return to the firehouse, knowing it's been another good day on the job.

Think About
the
Strategies

BEFORE READING

Preview the Selection
by looking at the title and headings to predict what the selection will be about.

 Write notes on your own paper to tell how you used this strategy.

DURING READING

Make Connections
by relating information that I already know about the subject to what I'm reading.

 When you come to a red button like this ⬤, write notes on your own paper to tell how you used this strategy.

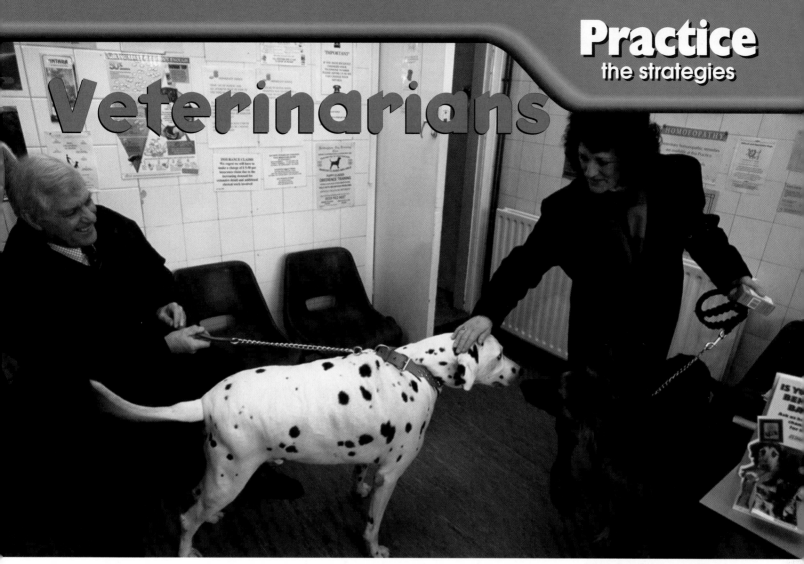

Veterinarians

Veterinarians care for many kinds of animals every day.

The students in class were worried. Something was wrong with Sneaker. The class pet had changed. The hamster seemed sick. He was sneezing. He had watery eyes.

The teacher took Sneaker to a veterinarian. A veterinarian, or "vet," is a doctor who treats animals. This vet sees dogs, cats, and birds in her office. She also cares for hamsters, gerbils, snakes, and many other kinds of animals.

A vet has many ways of telling if an animal is sick. Sometimes a vet listens to the owner. The owner tells how the animal has changed.

The vet can **examine** the animal by looking at him or her. The vet can also run different types of tests. Animals can have many of the same types of tests that humans have.

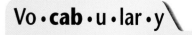

Vo•**cab**•u•lar•y

examine (ig•**zam**•in)—to look at carefully

Strategy

Make Connections by relating information that I already know about the subject to what I'm reading.

Write notes on your own paper to tell how you used this strategy.

What seems to be the problem?

After the animal is examined, the vet talks to the owner. Usually, a vet gives advice on how to care for the animal at home. For animals like dogs and cats, a veterinarian gives a **vaccination**. That stops the animal from getting an illness, such as **rabies**. Sometimes vets have to operate on animals.

With Sneaker, the vet said that the hamster had an **allergy**. She said the class should change Sneaker's bedding. What he sleeps on could cause the **reaction**. The class changed the type of bedding. Soon, Sneaker was healthy again. He did not sneeze anymore. His eyes did not water. Everyone was happy, especially Sneaker!

Training

Are you good in math and science? If you think you might want to be a vet someday, these would be good subjects to study. Vets have to be good at math and science. Vets need to know math and science because they must know how much medicine to give each animal. They must

Vo • **cab** • u • lar • y

vaccination (vak•suh•**nay**•shuhn)— an injection to protect against a disease

rabies (**ray**•beez)—an often fatal disease that can affect warm-blooded animals

allergy (**al**•uhr•jee)—a bad reaction to something, causing sneezing or a rash

reaction (ree•**ak**•shuhn)— a response to something

measure it just right. They also need to know the parts of animals' bodies. That's what animal science is all about.

Vets also must be caring people. We trust them to keep our pets happy and healthy.

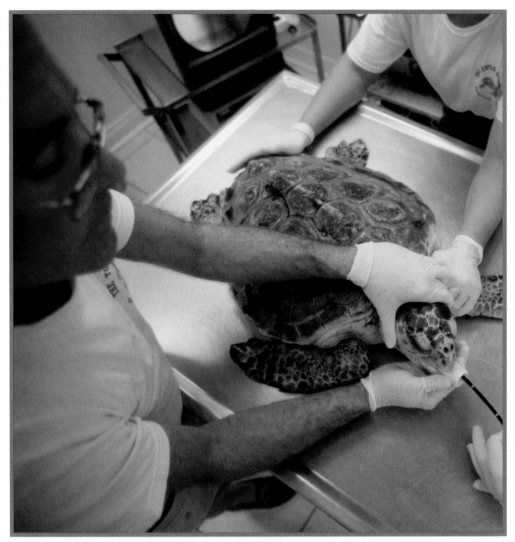

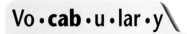
Vets need to learn how to cure all sorts of animals.

To become a vet, a man or a woman goes to a special school. Students study dogs, cats, turtles, snakes, horses, and birds. They study many kinds of animals.

In school, students learn many things. They go to class. They read long books. They learn how healthy animals look. They learn what animals need to stay healthy. They find out how to treat animals when they get ill. They learn how to draw blood for tests. They work with real animals. Vets also learn **communication** skills. Some students

Vo • **cab** • u • lar • y

communication
(kuh•myoo•ni•**kay**•shunh)
—exchange of thoughts, information, or ideas

[25]

Make Connections
by relating information that I already know about the subject to what I'm reading.

Write notes on your own paper to tell how you used this strategy.

learn about how to deal with **grief** and loss. They also learn about **ethics**. Students see their teachers and older students as role models. Learning from other students who have had experience is very important.

School is hard, but students learn a lot. After four years of college and then vet school, students graduate.

Types of Animals

Today, more than 60,000 vets work in the United States. That number might seem high to you. But many animals also live in this country. How many are there?

- 53 million dogs
- 59 million cats
- 13 million birds kept as pets
- 4 million horses that are kept for friendship (does not include working horses)
- almost 6 million rabbits and ferrets kept as pets

To keep these animals healthy, we need smart doctors who know what to do.

Which type of pet is most popular in the United States?

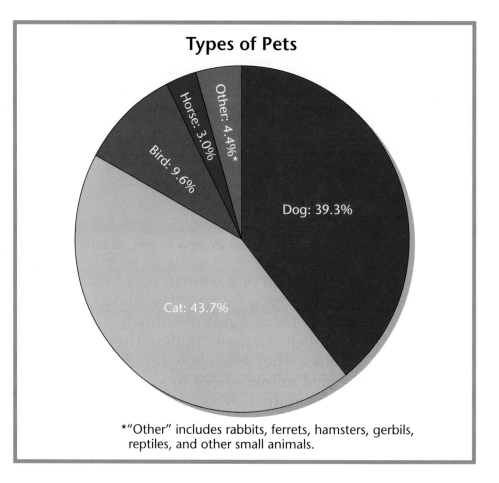

Types of Pets

Dog: 39.3%
Cat: 43.7%
Bird: 9.6%
Horse: 3.0%
Other: 4.4%*

*"Other" includes rabbits, ferrets, hamsters, gerbils, reptiles, and other small animals.

Vo·**cab**·u·lar·y

grief (greef)—great sadness

ethics (**eth**•iks)—a set of principles of right conduct; moral values

Kinds of Veterinarians

Most veterinarians work with small animals. But all sorts of animals may come through the door. Some of these animals walk. Others hop. Still others crawl. Many types of animals exist. Does the animal have four legs or two? Is it old or young? Does it have worms or fleas? No matter, the vets see them all.

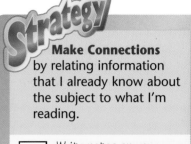

Strategy

Make Connections by relating information that I already know about the subject to what I'm reading.

Write notes on your own paper to tell how you used this strategy.

Vets see animals with special names. They meet "Elvis," a boxer who limps through the door on all fours. They examine "Spot," a lizard who comes through the door in a cage.

Vets say that some pet names are more popular than others. The favorite pet name in the United States is Max. Sam, Lady, Bear, and Smoky are also popular. These can be names for cats, rabbits, dogs, or birds.

Some vets work in zoos. They may treat an elephant with a cold or a tiger with a toothache. Or, they may see a lion that will soon have cubs. They may weigh a baby giraffe to see if he's growing right. Perhaps they fix a bird's broken wing.

Vets aim to stop the spread of disease to other animals and to humans.

Wildlife **rehabilitation** centers are places that rescue and treat wild animals, such as birds, foxes, and deer. Vets save injured animals and then release them back to their wildlife homes.

Some animals live on farms. Cows, pigs, horses, and chickens are just some of the animal doctor's **patients**. Some vets travel from one farm to another.

Vets check to be sure that the animals are fed right. They make sure the animals are clean. They don't want the animals to **spread** disease.

Vo•cab•u•lar•y

rehabilitation (ree•huh•bil•i•**tay**•shuhn)— the restoring of the sick or injured to good health

patients (**pay**•shuhnts)— anyone who receives treatment by a doctor

spread (spred)—to reach out over a wide area

Strategy

Make Connections by relating information that I already know about the subject to what I'm reading.

Write notes on your own paper to tell how you used this strategy.

Not every vet works only with animals. Some work to make better medicines for the animals. They develop new drugs. They try different things before they get it right.

Teaching is the main job of other vets. These animal doctors work in schools. They train the vets of tomorrow.

Joys and Dangers of the Job

Most veterinarians enjoy their work. They love animals. They love keeping animals healthy. They love making people happy by caring for the animals around them.

But some parts aren't much fun. A vet must be careful. Some animals don't like going to the vet. They get nervous. Sometimes they hurt the vet when they try to get away. Some animals may bite. Other animals kick. Still others scratch. The job can be dangerous that way.

Vets don't like it when an animal dies. Vets do all they can to save their patients. But some can't be saved.

Like other people, vets get tired. They may work long hours. They may want to spend more time at home. But they are needed at the office.

Still, vets take the good with the bad. It's what they do. Being a vet is an important job. As one vet says, "I wanted to be a veterinarian because I like animals. I wanted to be able to help them and their owners when they become sick. Vets help all kinds of animals and people. We have a very interesting job."

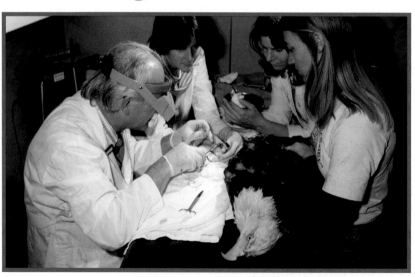

Veterinarians operate to save this eagle. When he is better he will be returned to his wildlife home.

Smart and Caring

Many veterinarians feel as if they have been called to do their work. They love animals and people. They want to provide the best care possible for their patients. That is why they study so hard in school. That is why they work through the hard times. They are able to **improve** the lives of the animals they treat. Just as in human medicine, improvements are being made all the time. Scientists and doctors work hard to improve medications and **procedures**. This will keep animals healthy and strong for longer periods of time. This makes the animals and their people happy. Vets are smart, **responsible,** caring people. If this describes you and you love animals, maybe you should consider becoming a veterinarian.

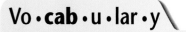

Vo·cab·u·lar·y

improve (im•**proov**)— to make better

procedures (pruh•**see**•juhrz) —ways of doing something or getting something done

responsible (ri•**spon**•suh•buhl)— dependable, trustworthy, reliable

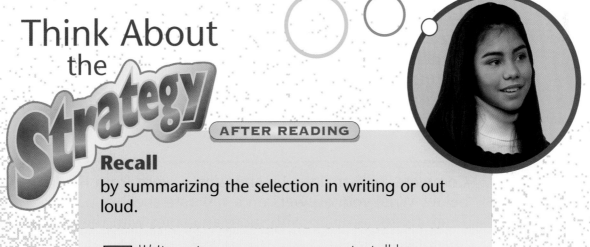

Think About the Strategy

AFTER READING

Recall

by summarizing the selection in writing or out loud.

Write notes on your own paper to tell how you used this strategy.

Analogies

In "Veterinarians," you learned that a vet may see a lion that will soon have cubs. *Lion* is the name for the adult. *Cub* is the name for the baby.

Read across to find other names for animals and their babies:

Type of Adult Animal	Baby
goat	kid
duck	duckling

One way to say Lines 1 and 2 is:
    Goat is the adult and *kid* is the baby.
    Duck is the adult and *duckling* is the baby.

A shorter way to say the same thing is:
    Goat is to *kid* as *duck* is to *duckling.*

This sentence is called an **analogy**. An analogy is a way of comparing things that may be related.

Complete each analogy by choosing a word from the list below. Write your answers on a separate sheet of paper. Then, try to come up with more analogies with the answers not used.

piglet   lamb   puppy   horse   chick   kitten   colt

1. *Lion* is to *cub* as *dog* is to _____.

2. *Cow* is to *calf* as *sheep* is to _____.

3. *Tiger* is to *cub* as *pig* is to _____.

4. *Chicken* is to *chick* as *cat* is to _____.

5. *Deer* is to *fawn* as *horse* is to _____.

Narrative

Practice reading this narrative about a trip to the vet to yourself. Rehearse using good phrasing and expression. When you're ready, read it aloud to the class.

Fluency TIP

As you read, be sure to express in your voice how worried Marissa is about Max. Also express how sure the doctor is that everything will be fine.

Yesterday, Mom, Dad, and I took Max to the vet. "What's the problem with your cat?" Dr. Cantor asked us when we got to the office.

I told Dr. Cantor that Max has been coughing and sneezing. He's been sleeping too much. He seems sad. "We're worried!" I said.

Dr. Cantor tried to pull Max out of his carrier. But Max dug in his claws and had to be pulled out of the box. Everyone laughed.

"I guess Max doesn't like to go to the doctor," said Dr. Cantor.

Dr. Cantor petted Max and scratched him behind the ears. I watched as Max quickly settled into a deep purr. I guess Max didn't think the vet was so bad, after all.

Next, the vet looked into Max's eyes. She saw that they were clear. She checked his teeth and gums. She felt all over Max's body.

"Everything looks good so far," the vet told us. Then she listened to Max's heart and lungs.

"Max's heart sounds fine. But he does have congestion in his lungs. I think Max has a cold."

"A cold?" I said.

"Oh, yes! Cats get colds sometimes, just like people do. We'll give Max some medicine. It will make him feel better. Before you know it, Max will seem just like himself."

The vet was right because Max said, "Purr!"

Think About the Strategies

BEFORE READING

Preview the Selection

by looking at the title and headings to predict what the selection will be about.

DURING READING

Make Connections

by relating information that I already know about the subject to what I'm reading.

AFTER READING

Recall

by summarizing the selection in writing or out loud.

 Use your own paper to jot notes to apply these Before, During, and After Reading Strategies. In this selection, you will choose when to stop, think, and respond.

Social Workers

Pat's father, Jonathan, walked into the school. He had a problem and needed to talk to the principal.

Jonathan told the principal that he was sick and needed an **operation**. It would take two months to get well. Who would care for Pat during that time? Who would cook her meals? Someone would have to take Pat to school. Jonathan was **worried**.

The principal knew what to do. She called a social worker. A social worker is someone who helps others. A social worker helps people solve problems. This social worker had an office in Pat's school.

Pat's social worker made some calls. She found a housekeeper to go to Pat's house. The housekeeper helped Pat get ready for school. The housekeeper cooked Pat's meals. She walked Pat to and from school.

Vo•cab•u•lar•y

operation
(op•uh•**ray**•shuhn)—surgery to fix a part of the body

worried (**wur**•eed)—concerned

[33]

Finally, Pat's father got well. So, the housekeeper went to a different family. Later, the social worker checked up on Pat's family. All was well. The social worker was able to help.

What Do Social Workers Do?

Social workers are people who want to improve others' lives. Their work can take many forms. Some assist the sick. They are not doctors. But they match the right doctor with the person who is ill.

Other social workers help people get jobs. One man wanted to be a cook. The social worker told him which school would prepare him for that job. Social workers also train people to find work. They give tests to help match people with jobs. They show people how to fill out important forms.

Social workers help people who have drug and alcohol problems. Together, they develop plans to get well. They set **goals**. Social workers refer people to doctors and counselors who will help them, too.

Social workers screen new patients.

As part of the job, social workers take good notes. They **interview** people. They jot things down on charts. They make calls. They keep records so that other helpers know what's going on. They make sure things get done.

Where Do Social Workers Work?

The United States has more than 800,000 social workers. In what **settings** can they be found?

One place social workers are needed is in nursing homes. As people grow older, sometimes they must move into a nursing home. Many older people have health problems. They might have cancer. They might suffer from heart disease. Or, they might be sad all the time.

At nursing homes, many doctors and nurses are able to care for older and sick people. Social workers work in nursing homes, too. They have many jobs. Meeting with families and arranging for doctor visits are just some of the things they do. Some social workers **counsel** their patients about their health and their new **surroundings**.

Social workers are also needed to work in the jail system. In the United States, there are almost 2 million people in our jails. Where will the ex-inmates live when they get out? What kinds of jobs will they have? Social workers set up job training to help inmates get ready for life outside the prison walls.

Is there a social worker in your school? If so, he or she makes sure all the students come to class. If a child has too many absences, social workers find out why. They take steps to bring the child back to class.

Some students have problems in the classroom. They may fight or cry a lot or sleep during lessons. They may get into trouble all the time. Or, they may be withdrawn. These children may need to see the school social worker. The social worker arranges for the student to get help. He or she might visit the home and counsel the whole family.

Social workers check on patients in nursing homes and hospitals.

The social worker needs to know why the child has been absent from school.

Vo•cab•u•lar•y

settings—places

counsel (**kown**•suhl)— to offer or give advice to

surroundings (suh•**round**•ings)— the environment around a person

Some social workers work in hospitals. One of the jobs in a hospital is to help people who suffer from drug or alcohol addictions. They help them to live a life without drugs. When social workers meet new patients, they talk to them about their goals. Together, they decide on the steps needed to reach those goals.

Hospital social workers work as part of a team. Doctors, nurses, and a clerical staff all work together. The team supports patients as they **recover** and refers them to other services, if needed. Sometimes a patient needs more schooling, such as a high school education. The team explains how to get a diploma. Many people are helped by the team's work. One hospital social worker said, "It's wonderful to see a person get healthier. It's like watching a flower opening up."

But the job has its tough parts. Some patients stay in treatment for a long time. But they do not get well. The team does its best to help as many patients as it can.

Social workers also work with families. We all want good mothers and fathers. But some parents aren't kind to their children. They put their children in danger. In those cases, a social worker finds a safe home for the children. Social workers visit the **foster** home to make sure the children are safe. They also **monitor** the parents to see if they are working hard to be better parents. Often, the foster home lasts until the parents prove they can care for their children safely.

A Case Study

Social workers aim to make people's lives better. They put their ideas to good use. Let's see how.

Rose is a child with few friends. She is shy. Rose was very sick for a long time. She missed a lot of school. Rose needs help learning to trust children her own age. She needs to learn to **socialize** with other children.

Rose has a social worker named Nick. Nick had an idea that might help Rose. Maybe she needed a different kind of friend. First, Nick made sure that Rose's family would provide a good home for a pet. Then, he suggested to Rose's mother that they get a dog. The whole family would be responsible for and enjoy the dog. But the pet would belong to Rose.

Dogs can bring out the best in people.

Vo·cab·u·lar·y

recover (ri•**kuv**•uhr)—to get better

foster (**faw**•stuhr)—giving or sharing care like that of a parent although not related by blood or adoption

monitor (**mon**•i•tuhr)—to keep watch over

socialize (**soh**•shuh•lyz)—to make friends; to gather with friends

Rose named her new dog Buddy. Rose fed Buddy and played with him. She gave Buddy lots of **attention**. And he gave Rose attention, too. Rose also walked Buddy twice a day. One day, Buddy licked another dog. Everyone laughed. With Buddy's help, Rose made new friends.

Every month, Rose's mother meets with Nick. They talk about how Rose is doing in school and at home. Rose's mother is happy to report, "Rose seems happier. She has more energy. She has made many new friends." Social workers know that pets improve people's lives.

Making It Better

Social workers are smart and responsible. They care a great deal for people. Sometimes their work is hard. They must be able to get along with many different people. Sometimes they have to deal with bad situations. But that is what they are there for. They are there to help make bad situations better. That is why they become social workers. As one social worker says, "I became a social worker because I wanted to help people. Some people do not have someone to help them through hard times. I wanted to be the person who could help. With a little help, many patients are able to meet their goals."

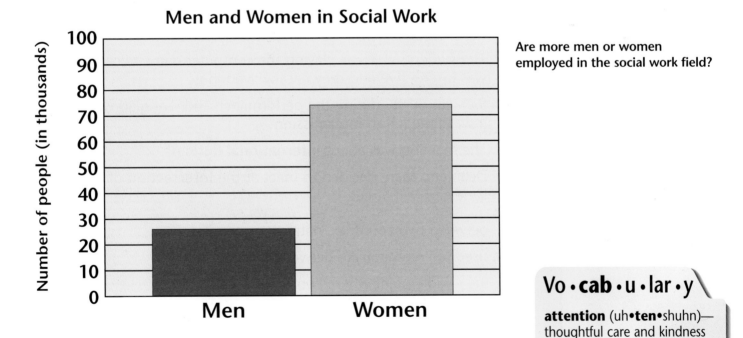

Men and Women in Social Work

Number of people (in thousands)

Men
Women

Are more men or women employed in the social work field?

Vo·**cab**·u·lar·y

attention (uh•**ten**•shuhn)—thoughtful care and kindness

[37]

Vocabulary

Word Parts

Inter- is a **word part** that means "between" or "in the middle of."

In "Social Workers," you read that a social worker may *interview* a client. *Interview* is made up of two word parts: *inter-* and *view*. In this case, *inter-* means "between." An *interview* is a meeting *between* two people.

Each of the following sentences has a word with the word part *inter-*. Therefore, the word has a meaning related to "between" or "in the middle of."

1. The police tried to **intercept** the robber.
   In this sentence, *intercept* means "to come in between or in the middle of the robber and where he was going."

2. Sally tried not to **interrupt** Tom's work.
   In this sentence, *interrupt* means "to come in between Tom and his work."

Read the following sentences, and then find the definition in the list below that matches the boldface word. Write your answers on a separate piece of paper. Then, write five new sentences using the boldface words.

1. The parents used the **intercom** in the family room to listen for their child's voice.

2. The students enjoyed playing the computer game because it was **interactive** and they felt involved in it.

3. Joel was thirsty during the performance and was glad when it was time for an **intermission**.

4. The meeting was about **international** business.

5. Dean and Mary decided to meet at the **intersection** of River Lane and Mill Street.

   a. between two countries, nations, or peoples

   b. used to communicate between two rooms

   c. the middle point where two roads meet

   d. to act between each other or between things

   e. a break between two acts in a play

Readers' Theater

You have read about social workers and their jobs. Read this script between the social worker and the family that you read about in the selection. Practice it so that you can read it with expression.

Fluency TIP

As you practice reading this, ask others to listen to you. Ask them to tell you what you did well in your reading and what you might do to make your reading even better.

Our Dog, Buddy

Narrator: Rose and her mother are walking their dog, Buddy. Nick, a social worker, is with them.

Nick: So, Rose, how are you and Buddy getting along?

Rose: Oh, I love him! He is my best friend!

Nick: That's why having pets is so great. When we treat them well, they want to be with us.

Rose's mom: It was hard when we first got Buddy. We weren't used to taking walks so often. But Buddy needs to get out of the apartment.

Nick: Dogs don't like to stay inside all the time. They need to see the world. And they need exercise, just like people.

Rose: I try to walk Buddy three times a day. I don't always feel like it. But Buddy makes me go out. I'm stronger because of our walks!

Rose's mom: It's true. Rose seems to be so much healthier. She can do things she couldn't do before Buddy came to live with us.

Nick: That's such good news! Pets *are* wonderful. They really can improve our lives. We care for them, and they care for us.

Rose: I was a little shy before I got Buddy. I was scared of seeing people. But now, with Buddy, I feel safe! People love to say hello to him. And they talk to me, too!

Nick: Rose, I'm so pleased for you and Buddy!

Buddy: Ruff!

Narrator: The social worker leaves as Rose and her family stand at the door of their apartment. Everyone agrees: It's been a happy day.

Steps in a Process

Fire Safety at Home

We all practice fire drills at school. But it is smart to have a plan for the home, too. You and your family should make a good escape plan in case of fires in your home. Each person in the family must know what to do if a fire occurs. But you must let the firefighters put out the fire.

How can you be safe from a fire in your home?

1 Your home should have loud smoke detectors. A smoke detector is the most important safety tool in the home. Ask your mom or dad to make sure they are in place.

2 The batteries in the smoke detectors should be checked each month.

3 The batteries in the smoke detectors must be changed two times each year. A good way to remember is to change them in April and October, when the clocks are changed.

4 Practice fire drills in the home. Everyone must know how to get out of the house safely.

5 Smoke is dangerous. Smoke rises in the air. Everyone must learn to crouch and crawl under the smoke.

6 Have a special meeting place outside of the house. Draw a map so everyone knows where to go.

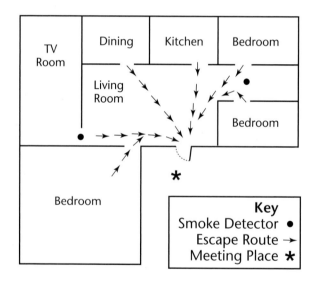

7 Everyone must know how to contact firefighters. Remember to call the numbers 9-1-1 for help. Practice saying your last name and street address.

These are good fire safety practices for home. Work with your family to make the plan. Then practice it once each month.

Discussion Questions

Answer these questions with a partner or on a separate piece of paper.

1. Why should the batteries in the smoke detectors be changed?
   a. Your parents can practice taking out batteries.
   b. New batteries make the smoke detectors work well.
   c. Smoke detectors use batteries.
   d. It is fun to change batteries.

2. What are the special numbers to call firefighters for help?
   a. Your phone number
   b. 1
   c. 9-1-1
   d. your age

3. Why should you have a special meeting place outside of the house?

4. Why must you crawl under the smoke of a fire?
   a. You get good exercise.
   b. A fire is hot.
   c. You crawl faster than you walk.
   d. Smoke is dangerous and rises.

5. Who is best at putting out a fire?

6. Why must you know your address?
   a. The firefighters need to find your house.
   b. You practice fire drills at that address.
   c. Smoke detectors must be in every home.
   d. Batteries must be checked.

7. Why should you practice saying your last name and address into the phone?
   a. The phone may not be working in a fire.
   b. People will be curious to know your name.
   c. You'll get it right in a real emergency.
   d. Talking on the phone is hard.

8. How often must the batteries in smoke detectors be changed?
   a. Batteries must be changed every month.
   b. Batteries are good for the life of the smoke detector.
   c. Batteries must be changed once every two years.
   d. Batteries must be changed two times per year.

CONNECTING
to the Real World

EXPLORE MORE

Write a Story
Write a story about your favorite pet. Add a picture or a drawing of your pet. Work with your mom or dad to send the story and picture to a veterinarian you know.

Conduct an Interview
Ask a firefighter to visit your class. He or she can talk about being a firefighter. Work with the class to develop a set of interview questions.

Make a Mask
Using a paper bag, make a mask of an animal. Color in whiskers and a nose. Cut out holes for the eyes and mouth. Use the mask to put on a play about veterinarians who help animals.

Conduct an Interview
Invite the social worker at your school to visit your classroom. Prepare a list of questions ahead of time. Interview this person about his or her job. Send a thank-you note after the visit.

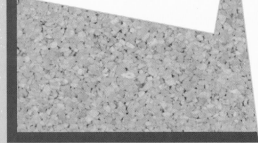

Research Careers
Research several careers that you find interesting. Write a short description of three of them. Then write why you are interested in these careers. Tell what kind of training or schooling is needed for each career. Tell about some of the good and bad points of each job. Use graphics if needed.

Create a Safety Display
Make drawings about fire safety with your friends in class. Write a sentence underneath each drawing. Ask your teacher to put them up around school. Your drawings will help other students think about fire safety.

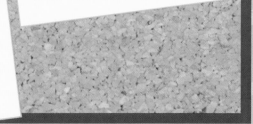

Related Books

Baglio, Ben M. *Kittens in the Kitchen (Animal Ark, No. 1).* Scholastic, 1998.

Demarest, Chris L. *Firefighters A to Z.* Margaret K. McElderry Books, Simon & Schuster, 2000.

Desimini, Lisa. *Dot the Fire Dog.* The Blue Sky Press, 2001.

Maze, Stephanie. *I Want to Be a Firefighter.* Harcourt Brace & Company, 1999.

—*I Want to Be a Veterinarian.* Harcourt Brace & Company, 1999.

Mitter, Matt. *Billy Blazes, Firefighter.* Reader's Digest Children's Books, 1999.

Owen, Ann. *Caring for Your Pets: A Book About Veterinarians.* Picture Window Books, 2003.

Simon, Charnan. *Jane Addams: Pioneer Social Worker (Community Builders).* Children's Book Press, 1998.

Interesting Web Sites

Firefighters

www.smokeybear.com

www.teacher.scholastic.com/commclub/firefighter/index.htm

Veterinarians

www.yahooligans.com/content/ask_earl/20020226.html

www.avma.org/careforanimals/kidscorner/default.asp

www.teacher.scholastic.com/commclub/vet/index.htm

Careers

www.kidsnewsroom.org/careers/careers.asp

www.whatdotheydo.com

Web sites have been carefully researched for accuracy, content, and appropriateness. However, teachers and caregivers are reminded that Web sites are subject to change. Internet use should always be monitored.

BEFORE READING

Activate Prior Knowledge

by looking at the title, headings, pictures, and graphics to decide what I know about this topic.

DURING READING

Interact With Text

by identifying the main idea and supporting details.

AFTER READING

Evaluate

by searching the selection to determine how the author used evidence to reach conclusions.

LEARN
the strategies
in the selection
The Dance of the Bees
page 47

PRACTICE
the *strategies*
in the selection
Our Friends, the Chimpanzees
page 59

APPLY
the *strategies*
in the selection
The Whales Around Us
page 69

Think About the Strategies

Activate Prior Knowledge

by looking at the title, headings, pictures, and graphics to decide what I know about this topic.

My Thinking

The strategy says to look at the title, headings, pictures, and graphics to decide what I already know about this topic. The title is "The Dance of the Bees." The first few heads are "The Meaning of the Dance," "Types of Bees," and "Worker Bees." All of these are about bees and what they do.

Now I'll look at the photos. I see photos of bees moving in some way. The graphic is a diagram of a bee moving on a certain path.

I predict that the selection will be about how and why bees move, and what it means. I'll read on to see if I'm right.

DURING READING

Interact With Text

by identifying the main idea and supporting details.

My Thinking

The strategy says to identify the main idea and supporting details. I will stop and think about this strategy every time I come to a red button like this ⦿.

THE DANCE OF THE BEES

Honeybees are one species of dancing bee.

Imagine this. Your brother walks in the house. He asks you where the oranges are. You spin around and wiggle. You jump up and down. Then you shake your hips and flap your arms. Your brother nods his head and says, "Oh, thanks." He pulls the delicious oranges out of the refrigerator. "No problem," you respond.

That is how some bees **communicate**. They tell each other very **specific** information through movement. That is how they talk about gathering food. They dance.

Vo•cab•u•lar•y

communicate
(kuh•**myoo**•ni•kayt)—
to exchange thoughts, ideas, or information

specific (spi•**sif**•ik)—
particular or exact

Strategy

Interact With Text by identifying the main idea and supporting details.

My Thinking

The main idea in this section is that there are different types of dances. The supporting details tell me one is for direction, another is for type of food, and a third is for how much food there is.

The Meaning of the Dance

One type of dance move tells the distance the bees are from food. Another move tells direction. Some moves tell other bees about the type of food. Other moves let the bees know how much food there is. The bees use a whole language of dance.

Types of Bees

Three types of bees live in a **hive**. There is the queen. She is the largest bee in the hive. The queen is the only female who can lay eggs. She can lay 3,000 eggs in one day. There are **drones**. Drones are all males. The drones have one job. They **mate** with the queen. Finally, there are worker bees. These bees use dance language. They have an important job. They feed all the other bees in the hive. Worker bees are all **infertile** females.

Vo•cab•u•lar•y

hive (hyv)—a structure built by bees and used as their home

drones (drohnz)—male insects who mate with the queen

mate (mayt)—to connect for breeding

infertile (in•**fur**•tl)—unable to create offspring

The queen is the biggest bee in the hive.

Worker Bees

Two kinds of worker bees are responsible for food. These are **scout** bees and **forager** bees. Scout bees fly around and search for food. They find a source of **nectar** or **pollen** and then fly back to the hive. In the hive, they go to a clear spot. Scientists call this area the "dance floor." There, bees perform their dance. The forager bees watch the show. When the bee ballet is over, the forager bees go out to find the food based on the scouts' dance. How does it work? Let's look at the different parts of the bees' dance language.

Strategy

Interact With Text by identifying the main idea and supporting details.

My Thinking
The main idea is that two kinds of worker bees are responsible for food. The supporting details are that the scout bees search for food. The forager bees go out to find the food based on the scouts' dance.

These bees have things to say.

Vo·**cab**·u·lar·y

scout (skowt)—one who goes out to find things

forager (for•ij•uhr)—one who goes out to get food

nectar (nek•tuhr)—a sweet liquid found in flowers

pollen (pol•uhn)—a powdery substance produced by flowers for reproduction

Dancing to Show Distance

Scouts use three **features** in their dance to communicate distance. They use the space on the dance floor, the speed of their dance, and different types of moves.

When the food is less than 300 feet away, the scout bee just moves around in a circle. This is called the round dance. The closer the food source is, the faster she dances. When the food is more than 300 feet away, she dances in a figure eight. This means that she moves around an area in two loops. The pattern she makes is **similar** to the shape of the number 8. Also, when the food is farther away, she waggles, or moves back and forth. This is called the waggle dance.

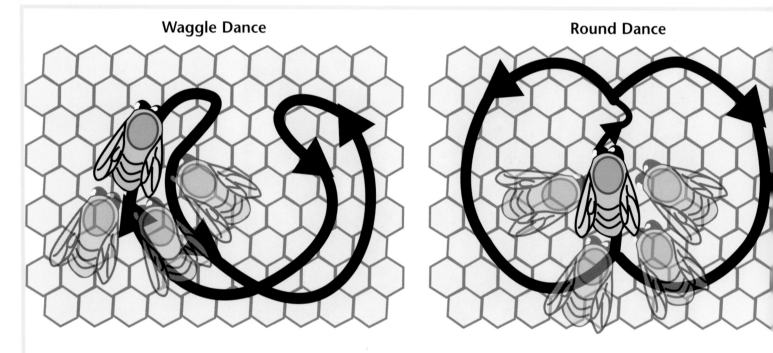

Waggle Dance

Round Dance

The waggle dance is for food sources that are farther away.
The round dance is done when food is close.

Vo·**cab**·u·lar·y

features (**fee**•chuhrz)—parts or details of something

similar (**sim**•uh•luhr)—like

theories (**thee**•uh•reez)—opinions or ideas based on observations

flicker (**flik**•uhr)—a quick and unsteady movement

How does the scout know the distance? Does she measure it? In a way, yes. Scientists used to think scouts did it by measuring the amount of energy they used to get there.

More recent **theories** suggest something else. Bees figure out the distance by receiving moving images while they fly. They see flowers bend. They see scenery change. This is called the **flicker** effect. When they see flowers moving in the breeze, they can tell they are covering distance.

Imagine being in a car. You are moving on a straight, empty highway. You are looking out the window. Everything looks the same. So, it is hard to tell how far you have gone. Now imagine that you are passing all sorts of interesting buildings and farms. It is easier to have a sense of how far you have gone. By looking at the sights as they fly, the bees can tell how far they have flown.

Direction

The scout tells the forager how far she has to fly. But which way? She needs to know direction. The scout uses the sun as a point of **reference**. She dances at an **angle** from the sun that copies the direction of the food source. If she dances at an angle west of the sun, then the food is to the west of the hive. Bees even have a sense of time. They change their dance as the sun changes positions throughout the day. They can do this without seeing the sun!

Bees in the hive cannot see the sun, but they still know what time of day it is.

Vo·cab·u·lar·y

reference (**ref**•uhr•uhns)— a point or spot used to help figure out location

angle (**ang**•guhl)—a slope off of a straight line

Interact With Text by identifying the main idea and supporting details.

My Thinking

The main idea is that scouts use repetition to tell how much food there is. The supporting detail is that the more the scout repeats the dance, the more food there is.

Amount of Food

Imagine that your father has two bags of groceries. You could probably help him by carrying them yourself. But if he has five bags, then you probably need more helpers. Likewise, the foragers pick up the food for the rest of the hive. So, they need to know how much food there is. The scouts tell them this by **repetition**. The more the scout repeats the dance, the more food there is. If the scout repeats the dance many times, then that means there is a lot of food.

A scout told this bee what to look for.

All in the Scent

Bees feed on different things. They get pollen and nectar from flowers and trees. The foragers need to know what to look for. The scouts' dance tells them. The scout was already at the food source. When she dances, she **releases** the scent of the food. Then the foragers seek that scent.

Vo•cab•u•lar•y

repetition (rep•i•**tish**•uhn)—something happening more than once

releases (ri•**lees**•ez)—lets out

Dancer Bees

Bees are interesting creatures. They do not just fly and sting. They are dancers and communicators. That makes them more like people. Bees dance as a form of **expression**. Bees have a form of expression all their own.

So, the next time your brother asks where the oranges are, think about the bees. Imagine you are a scout. Imagine how you would tell him there is one orange in the north corner of the refrigerator.

Vo·cab·u·lar·y

expression (ik•**spresh**•uhn)— showing thoughts or feelings

Think About the Strategy

AFTER READING

Evaluate

by searching the selection to determine how the author used evidence to reach conclusions.

My Thinking

The strategy says to evaluate by searching the selection to determine how the author used evidence to reach conclusions. This means I will decide how the author supported the conclusions.

Under the heading "Dancing to Show Distance," the author writes about what scientists thought. They thought scout bees measured distance with energy. But new theories suggest that the bees receive moving images as they fly. The author has checked scientific evidence and theories.

Graphic organizers help us organize information. I think this article can be organized by using a network tree. A network tree organizes information about a central idea. The central idea goes on the highest level. Details, questions, or ideas are written on the next level. Details about those ideas are written below them. Lines connect related items on different levels.

Network Tree

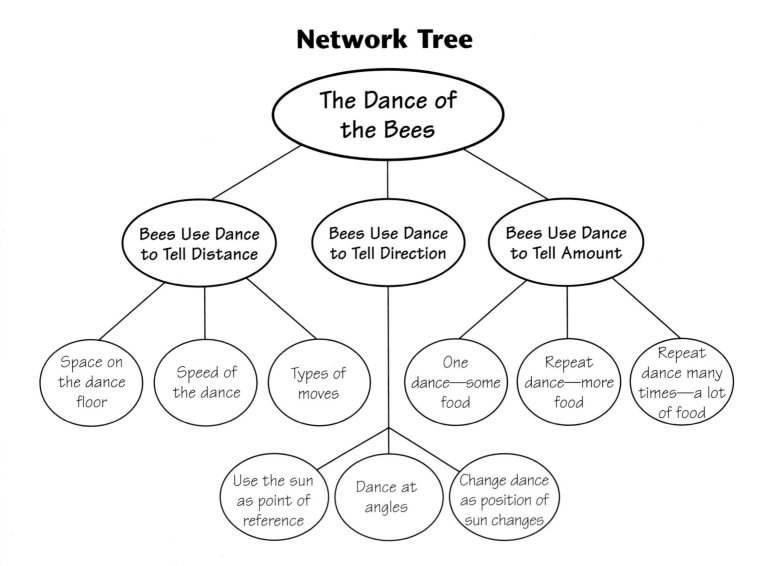

I used my graphic organizer to write a summary of the article. Can you find the information in my summary that came from my network tree?

A Summary of
The Dance of the Bees

Bees use the movements of dance to communicate with their hivemates. Different dance moves give different information, especially about food. One move tells the distance of the food. One move shows the direction of the food. Another move says how much food there is.

Bees use space, speed, and types of dance moves to communicate about the distance of food. If a bee dances in a close circle and doesn't use much space, then the food is close. If a bee dances fast, then that also means the food is close. If a bee waggles, which is a type of dance, then that means the food is farther away.

Bees use a dance to help them tell the direction of their food. They use the sun as a point of reference. Bees dance at an angle to the sun to show the direction of the food source. Then the other bees will follow that angle. Bees will change the angle and type of dance as the sun changes positions as the day goes on. This will tell the other bees in the hive what time of day it is and also where to find the food.

The dance of the bees also tells how much food they will find. If a bee only dances one dance, there is not much food. She probably doesn't need help with it. If the bee repeats her dance once, she might need a little help carrying the food. If a bee dances many times, she will need a lot of help!

Bees communicate very important information. Communicating about food is important to their survival. Bees use beautiful dances to communicate and express themselves. They have that in common with humans!

Introduction
Here is how I developed my introductory paragraph. It gives readers an idea of what they are about to read.

Body
I used information from each arm of the network tree for each paragraph in the body of my paper. The first body paragraph tells about distance. The second tells about direction. And the third body paragraph tells about the amount of food.

Conclusion
I summarized my paper by recalling the main ideas.

Compound Words

A **compound word** is a word that is made up of two smaller words. You can often figure out the meaning of the compound word by looking at the smaller words.

In "The Dance of the Bees," you read the compound word *honeybees.*

> **Honeybees** *are one species of dancing bee.*

Read these other compound words that are related to animals. Think about their meanings.

horse + shoe = horseshoe—a U-shaped iron plate fitted to a horse's hoof
grass + hopper = grasshopper—an insect with two pairs of wings and long hind legs used for jumping
bird + seed = birdseed—seeds for feeding birds
bird + house = birdhouse—a box with small holes used as a nesting place for birds
gold + fish = goldfish—a fish that is gold in color

Choose a word from Column 1 to add to a word in Column 2 to make a new compound word. Write the new words on your own paper. Then, write the dictionary definition for each compound word.

Column 1	Column 2
a. neck	**1.** _____ + hound
b. bull	**2.** _____ + dog
c. tail	**3.** cow + _____
d. blood	**4.** turtle + _____
e. bell	**5.** pig + _____

Poetry

A cinquain is a five-line poem. By yourself, practice reading these cinquains about bees. Practice reading them smoothly—let the words flow. This is using good fluency and expression. When you're ready, read them aloud to the class.

Fluency

▶ TIP

As you practice the poems the second time, try reading the lines differently. Say some words louder and some softer. Read some words faster and some slower. Does changing how you read each poem change its meaning?

Scout Bee Cinquain

Scout Bee
Dance straight, dance down,
Targets, pinpoints, angles
Excellent honeycomb worker
Hivemate

Worker Bee Cinquain

Workers
Busy, Dancers
Forage, waggle, circle
Transmit the flowers' source
Nature

Queen Bee Cinquain

Queen Bee
Hive's egglayer
Feeds, Breeds, Mothers
Can lay three thousand in a day
Honey

Think About
the
Strategies

Activate Prior Knowledge

by looking at the title, headings, pictures, and graphics to decide what I know about this topic.

 Write notes on your own paper to tell how you used this strategy.

DURING READING

Interact With Text

by identifying the main idea and supporting details.

 When you come to a red button like this ⦿, write notes on your own paper to tell how you used this strategy.

Our Friends, THE CHIMPANZEES

Chimpanzees are more like people than any other animal.

Two **chimpanzees** sit in a field of grass. One chimp lies on its back. The other chimp sits nearby. He runs his fingers gently through the first chimp's hair. Soon the chimps change places. It is the second chimp's turn to be stroked. It feels good and both chimps are happy. This is one way that chimps show friendship to each other. It is one way they communicate.

Chimpanzees are smart animals. They communicate in many ways. Scientists have studied the ways that chimps communicate for many years. At first, scientists only studied how chimps communicated in laboratories. But study like this is not good. Taking the chimps out of their **habitat** is unfair treatment. And the scientists could not get a true look at their real **behavior** in their own habitat. Scientists didn't know how chimps communicated in the forests where they lived.

Vo · **cab** · u · lar · y

chimpanzees (chim•pan•**zeez**)— small, hairy animals that are part of the ape family

habitat—the place where an animal or plant naturally lives and grows

behavior (bi•**hayv**•yuhr)— how something acts or reacts

Strategy

Interact With Text by identifying the main idea and supporting details.

Write notes on your own paper to tell how you used this strategy.

Learning About Chimps

Jane Goodall is an **expert** on chimps. She was one of the first people to begin to find out how chimps communicate when they live in the forest.

Goodall started to study chimpanzees in 1960. She knew nothing about them then. But she wanted to learn. She just had to get close enough to watch them.

It was hard for Goodall to study the chimps. She had to go to Africa. The chimps lived deep in the forest there. She climbed up **cliffs** to find them. She walked for miles in the forest. When Goodall found a group of chimps, she watched them through the trees. She stayed very still, so they could not see her. She did not want to scare them away.

Jane Goodall has studied chimps in the forests of Africa for more than 40 years.

It took a long time. But Goodall found a way to get close to the chimps. She knew chimps liked bananas. So she offered them some. They came close to Goodall to get the fruit. Soon the chimps got used to Goodall. They were not scared of her anymore. They let her follow them around. They even let her touch them.

Goodall got close enough to study the chimps. She traveled with the chimps in the forest. She watched them each day and learned how they lived. She saw what they ate. She saw them hunt and use tools. She began to understand how chimps communicate with each other. And she had great **respect** for them. She taught us a lot of what we know about chimps today.

Vo・cab・u・lar・y

expert (**ek**•spurt)—a person who knows a lot about something

cliffs (**klifs**)—high walls of rock that have straight sides

respect (ri•**spekt**)—a feeling of regard or consideration

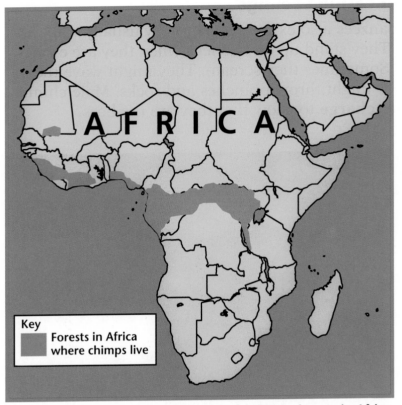

Chimpanzees live in forests in Africa.

Strategy

Interact With Text by identifying the main idea and supporting details.

Write notes on your own paper to tell how you used this strategy.

Why Chimps Communicate

We now know that chimps live in groups. We know they communicate to work together. They give each other information. They can communicate feelings. They can show friendship.

Communication for Food

Chimpanzees work together to find food. Communication helps them. The chimps might find a tree with many nuts. Each chimp does a job to get the nuts for the group. Some chimps climb into the trees. They shake the branches. The other chimps wait on the ground. They pick up the nuts that fall. Some chimps crack the nutshells. They take out the meat and share it. Young chimps sit and watch. They learn how to crack the nuts.

Chimps can also tell others when they find a big supply of food. They'll jump through trees and hoot loudly. They'll beat on the trunks of trees. Other chimps hear the noise. They follow the calls to find the food.

Communicating Feelings

Chimpanzees also express anger. They usually walk on all fours. They stand up on two legs when they are excited or angry. Sometimes they scream. They might wave their arms. They might throw branches and rocks. Male chimps sometimes **charge** to show that they are the boss.

Chimps groom each other for about one hour each day.

Showing Friendship

Grooming is an important part of communication for chimps. It shows friendship. When chimps **groom** each other, they pick things out of each other's hair. They take out dirt, insects, and leaves. Chimps spend about an hour each day in friendly activities, such as grooming.

Strategy

Interact With Text by identifying the main idea and supporting details.

Write notes on your own paper to tell how you used this strategy.

Vo•**cab**•u•lar•y

charge —to run toward something

groom—to clean, brush, and make something look neat

[62]

Chimps use many sounds to communicate.

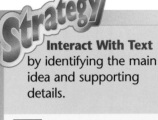

Strategy

Interact With Text by identifying the main idea and supporting details.

Write notes on your own paper to tell how you used this strategy.

How Chimps Communicate

Chimps use sound, movement, and facial expressions to communicate. They have a very special language. Chimps communicate with many sounds. They bark. They grunt. They scream. They make a long, loud sound when danger is near. That sound warns other chimps to stay away from an area. Each chimp has his or her own call, just as each person has a different voice. Chimps that live in the same group know each other's call. When they hear a call in the forest, they know who it is.

Chimps communicate by the way they hold their bodies. They also make **gestures** with their hands. Chimps greet each other by touching. They hug each other. They touch different parts of each other's bodies. When chimps greet an important member of their group, they show respect. Chimps with lower **rank** go up to the higher-ranked chimps. They crouch or hold out a hand. The higher-ranked chimps then touch the other chimps gently. They kiss or hug the chimps with lower rank. This lets the other chimps know that they are accepted. They are friends.

Chimps use their faces to communicate, too. A chimp's face can show excitement and fear. Chimps frown when they are angry. When they are afraid, some chimps will grin.

Vo·cab·u·lar·y

gestures (jes·chuhrz)—movements of parts of the body to communicate something

rank (rangk)—position in a group

[**63**]

Teaching Chimps to Communicate Like People

Scientists have studied chimpanzee communication for more than 40 years. They still study chimpanzee communication today. They have taught some chimps sign language. A chimp named Washoe learned 151 signs. A chimp named Lana learned symbols on a computer keyboard. She used the symbols to ask for food.

Can chimps learn to understand English? Some scientists think so. A chimp named Kanzi learned about 500 words. When a researcher said a word, Kanzi picked out the symbol for it on a keyboard.

Saving Chimps

We are still learning new things about how chimpanzees communicate. Some chimps have done amazing things. But chimps are in danger. Chimpanzees live in forests. People have cut down many of the forests where the chimps live. Many chimps have lost their homes and food supplies. Some people hunt chimps for meat, too. Chimps are gone in some places. Other places have fewer chimps than in the past.

Many people think we should protect the forests where chimps live. We know that chimps can communicate with people. Some of them even understand language. That makes them seem almost like us. With our help, chimpanzees will be around to "talk" to us for years to come.

National parks in Africa protect some groups of chimps.

All About Chimpanzees

Where they live: Forests in Africa

How tall they get: 28–38 inches

How much they weigh: 60–150 pounds

What they eat: Mostly fruit, leaves, seeds, stems, insects,
                         bird eggs; sometimes small animals and birds

How long they live: Up to 45–50 years in the wild

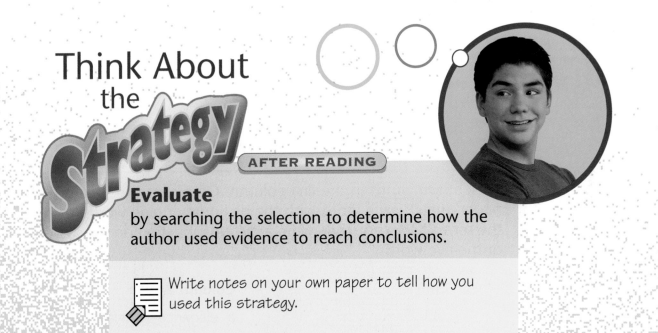

Think About
the
Strategy

AFTER READING

Evaluate
by searching the selection to determine how the author used evidence to reach conclusions.

Write notes on your own paper to tell how you used this strategy.

Vocabulary

Guide Words

Guide words are the words at the top of each page in a dictionary. They give the first and last entry words on the dictionary page.

Guide words appear in the dictionary to help you find entry words. If you want to find the meaning of *expert,* for example, you would start in the "e" section of the dictionary. Glancing at the guide words at the top of those pages, you would find a page with the guide words *exile* and *export. Expert* would appear somewhere on that page because *expe* comes after *exi* (in *exile*) and before *expo* (in *export*).

In "Our Friends, the Chimpanzees," you may have come across some words that were not defined in the selection. If you were to look them up in the dictionary, you would use guide words to help you find them.

exile   **export**

exist   expand
exit   expect
exodus   explore

Look at the words in the first column. On a separate sheet of paper, match each word with the dictionary guide words in the second column. Then write a dictionary definition for each of the five words.

Column 1

1. bald
2. elevate
3. gush
4. knight
5. praise

Column 2

a. elegance . . . eleventh
b. power . . . prance
c. knee . . . knot
d. bake . . . ball
e. gulch . . . gust

Letter

With a classmate, practice reading this exchange of letters between a young student and Dr. Jones, an expert on chimpanzees. Rehearse using good phrasing and expression. When you're ready, read it aloud to the class.

When reading the words of Dr. Jones, be sure to use confidence and authority in your voice—sound like an expert.

A Letter to Dr. Jones

Dear Dr. Jones,

How do chimpanzees groom each other? Why do they groom each other?

—Ana

Dear Ana:

Grooming serves two purposes for chimps.

First, it helps keep them clean, which is good for their health. In the forest, chimpanzees pick up lots of dirt, insects, and leaves in their hair. They groom by sitting next to each other and picking these things out of one another's hair. Chimps spend about an hour each day grooming!

Second, it is a way that chimpanzees communicate. They sit together and take turns grooming, which shows friendship. You know how nice it feels when your mother combs your hair and runs her fingers through it? That might be how grooming feels to chimps. It's relaxing, and it is a way for chimps to show that they care about the rest of their group.

Sincerely,

Dr. Jones

Think About the Strategies

BEFORE READING

Activate Prior Knowledge

by looking at the title, headings, pictures, and graphics to decide what I know about this topic.

DURING READING

Interact With Text

by identifying the main idea and supporting details.

AFTER READING

Evaluate

by searching the selection to determine how the author used evidence to reach conclusions.

 Use your own paper to jot notes to apply these Before, During, and After Reading Strategies. In this selection, you will choose when to stop, think, and respond.

The Whales Around Us

A dolphin is one type of whale.

The Clark family took a trip on the ocean. They sat on the boat. It was silent everywhere. Suddenly, they heard sounds. *Click, click, click.* They heard it again. *Click, click, click.* What or who was making those sounds? *Why* was it making those sounds?

The sounds were made by whales. Whales use sound to communicate with each other. But scientists say that whales communicate with each other in other ways, too. Besides sound, whales communicate by the way they act.

Shush! Is That a Whale?

Many whales make sounds. Some whales click. Some moan. Some even sing. Other whales whistle or bark.

How do whales make these sounds? They do not have **vocal cords** in their throat like humans. But, some whales do have **muscles** near a little spout or hole on the top of their head. That's where the clicking sounds are made. But those clicks are not just for communicating.

Is That an Echo? (Echo? . . . Echo?)

When a whale's click hits an object out in the ocean, the sounds bounce back to the whale's ears. It's like an echo. Scientists call this **echolocation**. Echolocation tells the whale if the object that the click has bounced off of is big or small, close or far away. It tells the whale if the object is moving or standing still. Echolocation helps the whale find food and other whales.

With echolocation, sounds bounce back to the whale, giving him important information.

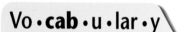

Vo·**cab**·u·**lar**·y

vocal cords (**voh**•kuhl **kordz**) —flaps or folds in the larynx (part of the windpipe) that help a person talk

muscles (**mus**•uhlz)—types of body tissue that produce motion

echolocation (ek•oh•loh•**kay**•shuhn)— a function in some animals in which high-pitched sounds are made and their echoes tell the direction and distance of objects

surface (**sur**•fuhs)—top layer

patterns (**pat**•uhrnz)— regular designs or arrangements

Underwater Chatter

Scientists think whales can communicate with each other as a group. Scientists saw whales gathering on the **surface** of the ocean. Then, they heard the whales make clicks in regular **patterns**. One whale would stop after a series of clicks. Then another whale made a series of clicks—and then another. This appeared to the scientists like people having a conversation. It seemed like people talking on the phone. But, what were the whales saying to each other? Perhaps they were just saying "Hello." Or, maybe they were planning their next meal.

What's for Dinner?

Whales communicate with each other in order to eat. Many whales travel in groups. Sometimes these groups are just a small family with a father (called a bull), a mother (called a cow), and a baby (called a calf). This family is called a pod.

A pod of dolphins

Sometimes whales travel in larger groups. Hundreds of whales may travel together. As they swim through the ocean searching for fish, they keep in contact with each other using different kinds of clicks and sounds.

When they locate their **prey,** they spring into action. They make a circle around the fish. The fish are trapped in the middle of the whales. The fish can't swim away. The whales grab the fish or slap them with their powerful tails, knocking them out. The whales then settle down to eat. By working together as a team, the whales can feed themselves. But it's not just with sounds that whales communicate.

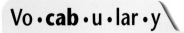

Whales work together to feed.

Vo·**cab**·u·lar·y

prey (pray)—an animal taken by another for food

[71]

Body Language

Whales also communicate by moving their bodies. Experts say that the way a whale behaves sends messages to other whales.

One body movement is called breaching. When a whale breaches, it leaps out of the water. It twists. Finally, it lands back in the water with a splash. Scientists have noticed that whales often breach when they are near other whales. The splash can be so loud that whales miles away hear it. So, experts say that the splash is a signal to other whales. Breaching might be a way of saying "Let's play!" or "Where's Charlie?" But we are still not sure. It might not be saying anything at all. Someday we hope to know for sure what breaching means.

A breaching whale

Whales can also communicate **aggressive** behaviors with their bodies. Scientists have seen whales ram other whales with their heads. They've seen whales kick other whales with their tails. And, they have seen whales **butt** others with their noses. What is the whale trying to say with this **rough** behavior? Experts think the whale is angry. Or maybe it's fighting for food. Perhaps it's warning another whale to keep away. Maybe the bull (the male) is telling another, "That cow (female) is with *me!*"

Vo·cab·u·lar·y

aggressive (uh•gres•iv)— forceful, bold

butt—to hit or push

rough (ruf)—not gentle or careful

When scientists studied dolphins "in the wild," they saw male dolphins slap their tails on the water. Their actions might be telling other dolphins to keep away from their food or their mate.

Studying and Saving Whales

Scientists do not have all the answers about *how* whales communicate. Studying whales can be hard. Because whales are so big, most research must be done in the ocean. Sometimes whales are hurt or even die. Some organizations are working hard to find ways to study whales without harming them. They study whales in **sanctuaries,** areas where they are protected.

Scientists can then study whales' **evolution,** behavior, and social life. And they can learn more about their communication. They put **microphones** in the water. They record the sounds. Then they study them to try to find patterns.

Someday scientists will have more answers. Hopefully, they will learn and will find ways to protect whales from **pollutants,** fishing nets, and other threats.

Meanwhile, if you're ever out on the ocean and hear strange clicking sounds, you might not be **imagining** things. It might just be a friendly whale saying "Hello!"

Some whales slap their tails on the water as a warning.

Scientists use special instruments to study whales in their habitat.

Vo·cab·u·lar·y

sanctuaries (**sangk**•choo•er•eez)—areas where animals and birds are protected

evolution (ev•uh•**loo**•shuhn) —gradual change or development

microphones (**my**•kruh•fohnz)— instruments for making sounds louder

pollutants (puh•**loot**•nts) —things that are unclean or harmful

imagining (i•**maj**•in•ing) —picturing in your mind

Context Clues

You can often figure out the meaning of an unfamiliar word by looking for other words or ideas in the sentence that are related to the unfamiliar word. This gives you a good clue as to the meaning of the word you don't know. This is called using **context clues**.

In "The Whales Around Us," you read this passage:

*They do not have **vocal cords** in their throat like humans.*

The word *throat* in the sentence helps you understand that **vocal cords** might be something found in one's throat.

Read these sentences from the selection. Notice the word or words in italics that help you get the meaning of the unfamiliar word in boldface.

1. When scientists studied dolphins "in the wild," they saw male dolphins **slap** their tails on the water. Their *actions* might be telling other dolphins to keep away from their food or their mate.

2. They put **microphones** in the water. They *record* the sounds.

3. This appeared to the scientists like people having a **conversation**. It seemed like people *talking on the phone*.

Write the following sentences on your own sheet of paper. For each sentence, underline the word or words that give a hint as to the meaning of the unfamiliar word in boldface.

1. The choir members sang beautifully, following the lead of the **conductor**.

2. "No, no, no!" said John. "I **refuse** to go to the office!"

3. The player ran to second base **rapidly**. The other team was not expecting him to run so fast.

4. I must return this **damaged** television set to the store because the knob is broken.

5. "Let's play **leapfrog**," said Mary. "We can jump over each other until we get to the other end."

Readers' Theater

You have finished reading an article about how whales communicate. With two partners, practice reading the script about marine biologists who are studying whale sounds. Rehearse using good phrasing and expression.

Fluency ▸ TIP

After practicing with your partners, change parts. Be sure to change how you read your part to reflect the character's personality.

Whale Watchers

Narrator: Two scientists are on a ship in the Pacific Ocean, off the coast of California. A pod of whales is swimming by. The scientists are listening to the whales' sounds through microphones placed under the surface of the water.

Dr. Singh: Listen to all those clicks! This is a very exciting study we are doing. The whales are using echolocation.

Dr. Quinn: Yes, I can hear the echoes. They seem to be talking a lot! They've probably run across some food source.

Narrator: Both scientists laugh. Whales are big animals; they need to eat a lot to stay alive. Some whales eat fish. They must always be looking out for prey.

Dr. Singh: Yes, they're saying, "Hey, Jane, look! There's lunch!"

Narrator: For a while, everyone is quiet. They listen through their headphones to hear what is being sent over the microphones. They keep watching the part of the ocean where the pod was last seen. Suddenly, a whale leaps out of the water and lands with a splash.

Dr. Singh: Whoa! That was amazing! Did you see that whale breach?

Dr. Quinn: He jumped really, really high! He must have had something important to communicate to the others in the pod.

Dr. Singh: Or else he was just having fun.

Dr. Quinn: Very possible! And we're lucky we get to study these amazing animals of the sea!

List

Help Save Endangered Animals

Earth is home to many endangered animals. Endangered animals must be protected and saved for future generations to enjoy.

Many things put these animals in danger. These are habitat destruction, pollution, and too much hunting.

What can you do to help endangered animals? You can

 Visit and support national parks, which protect wild animals and their homes.

 Make a home for butterflies in your own back yard. Work with an adult to create the right habitat.

 Organize a cleanup day at your local beach or park.

 Visit zoos and learn more about ways to keep animals safe.

 Make a presentation to the whole school. Try to get other children involved in helping endangered animals.

 Start a recycling project in your neighborhood.

 Build a bird feeder for your back yard.

 Volunteer at the local veterinarian's office. Learn as much as you can about animals while you help.

 Join, or start, a conservation club in your school or community.

Encourage your family and friends to buy "animal-friendly" products.

Many endangered animals can have a chance at longer and better lives on Earth with the help and support of all of us.

Discussion Questions

Answer these questions with a partner or on a separate sheet of paper.

1. What things can put animals in danger?

2. Where can you learn more about animals?
   a. habitats
   b. zoos
   c. Earth
   d. neighborhood

3. Why must we save endangered animals?

4. Why must we recycle?

5. What is an animal's habitat?
   a. its home
   b. its food
   c. its baby
   d. its mate

6. Why should we support national parks?

7. What is one thing you probably won't learn by talking to a vet?
   a. how dogs communicate
   b. how long big cats live
   c. where to buy a cot
   d. why some animals become extinct

8. Why is it valuable to volunteer at a veterinarian's office?
   a. to stay busy
   b. to make money
   c. to stop people from wasting energy
   d. to help animals and to learn about animals

EXPLORE MORE

Draw a Picture

Make a colorful drawing of the parts of a flower. Highlight or mark the parts where buzzing bees find pollen and food.

Let's Watch Videos

Host a video party to learn about chimpanzees. The animated movies "Tarzan" and "Aladdin" have humorous scenes that show how friendly chimpanzees can be and how humanlike they are.

Put on a Play

Make simple sock puppets, using magic markers to draw in the faces of different animals. Write and perform plays with the "animals" talking.

Write a Story

Write about how a whale comes upon a boat that is about to sink. The boat is full of people. Discuss how the whale tries to save the people. Maybe the whale makes sounds that call to other whales for help, or maybe the whale tows the boat to safety.

Do Research

Read books and magazines about animals. Or, use the Internet to find out how humans and chimpanzees are alike and different. Make a chart with the headings "Humans" and "Chimpanzees." Learn more about how animals such as whales, chimpanzees, and bees communicate.

Make a Calendar

Find pictures of 12 different kinds of whales, one for each month of the year. Make a calendar, and place a picture on each month.

Related Books

Facklam, Margery, and Pamela Johnson. *Bees Dance and Whales Sing: The Mysteries of Animal Communication.* Sierra Club Books, 2001.

Gates, Phil. *Animal Communication.* Cambridge University Press, 1997.

Goodall, Jane. *The Chimpanzee Family Book.* Michael Neuqebauer Books/ North–South Books, 1989.

—*The Chimpanzees I Love: Saving Their World and Ours.* Scholastic Press, 2001.

Jenkins, Steve. *Slap, Squeak, and Scatter: How Animals Communicate.* Houghton Mifflin Co., 2001.

Kalman, Bobbie. *How Animals Communicate (Cranapples).* Crabtree Publications, 1996.

Lewiston, Wendy Cheyette. *Buzz Said the Bee (Hello Reader, Level 1).* Scholastic Inc., 1992.

Lucas, Eileen. *Jane Goodall: Friend of the Chimps.* The Mill Brook Press, 1992.

Osborne, Mary Pope. *Good Morning, Gorillas (Magic Tree House, 26).* Random House, 2002.

Interesting Web Sites

Bees

www.pollinator.com/identify/whatsbuzzin.htm

www.pbs.org/wgbh/nova/bees/

Chimpanzees

www.janegoodall.org/chimps/communication.html

www.enchantedlearning.com/subjects/apes/chimp/index.shtml

Whales/Dolphins

http://newport.pmel.noaa.gov/whales/whale-calls.html

www.enchantedlearning.com/subjects/whales/

The Sounds of Many Animals

www.georgetown.edu/faculty/ballc/animals/animals.html

Web sites have been carefully researched for accuracy, content, and appropriateness. However, teachers and caregivers are reminded that Web sites are subject to change. Internet use should always be monitored.

Unit 3 Strategies

BEFORE READING

Set a Purpose

by using the title and headings to write questions that I can answer while I am reading.

DURING READING

Clarify Understanding

by using photographs, charts, and other graphics to help me understand what I'm reading.

AFTER READING

Respond

by drawing logical conclusions about the topic.

LEARN the *strategies* in the selection **The Wonders of Cirque du Soleil** *page 83*

PRACTICE
the **strategies**
in the selection
Racing in the Ironman
page 95

APPLY
the **strategies**
in the selection
The Special Olympics
page 105

Think About
the
Strategies

BEFORE READING

Set a Purpose

by using the title and headings to write questions that I can answer while I am reading.

My Thinking

The strategy says to use the title and headings to write questions that I can answer while I am reading. Part of the title, The Wonders of Cirque du Soleil, does not look like English. The questions I have are: What language is this? What does Cirque du Soleil mean in English?

I see that some headings are: "Welcome!," "The Acts," "The Studio in Montreal," "Behind the Scenes," "Giving and Teaching," and "Circus of Dreams Comes True." Some of my questions are: What kind of acts are they talking about? What goes on in The Studio in Montreal? What dreams have come true? Now I'll read on.

DURING READING

Clarify Understanding

by using photographs, charts, and other graphics to help me understand what I'm reading.

My Thinking

The strategy says to use photographs, charts, and other graphics to help me understand what I'm reading. I will stop and think about this strategy every time I come to a red button like this ⊙.

The Wonders of Cirque du Soleil

What is the acrobat doing?

Welcome!

People watch the show. A man stands on stage. The man bends backward. His body makes an **arc**. His head touches the floor. He pokes his head out through his legs.

The **audience** giggles. People are puzzled. Is this a real person? Can someone really fold back like that?

He creeps around the stage. He is bent backward the whole time. He acts just like a spider. He climbs onto a big block. Then he climbs off. He creeps around on his palms and his feet. He pokes his head out between his legs. He smiles. He pokes his head back in. It is a teasing smile. It is a spider smile.

Yes, a person can fold back like that. The man is a good **acrobat**. He is also a good actor. He makes everyone believe he is a spider. He is part of Cirque du Soleil (Surk du Soh•**lay**). This circus has clowns and acrobats. But no animals perform.

Vo • **cab** • u • lar • y

arc (ark)—upside-down "U" shape

audience (aw•**dee**•uhns)— people watching a show

acrobat (ak•ruh•bat)— a person who is skilled in stunts such as bending, swinging, and balancing

Strategy

Clarify Understanding
by using photographs, charts, and other graphics to help me understand what I'm reading.

My Thinking
This photograph shows me exactly what their tent looks like. I wonder what is happening inside?

Circus of the Sun

Cirque du Soleil is a special kind of circus. It has always been different. In the beginning, there wasn't even a circus tent. The circus was outside. It was held on the street. *Cirque du Soleil* means "Circus of the Sun." Can you figure out why it was named that? Because the street was the performer's stage, the sun lit their **acts**. Outside in the sunshine, the performers put on their show. They juggled. They did somersaults. They walked on **stilts**. Clowns ran around and acted crazy. Acrobats flipped. They wore amazing clothes. They bent their bodies into strange shapes. People in the street stopped. Everyone wanted to watch. It was hard just to walk by and not look.

Today, some things have changed. The performers don't perform in the street anymore. The circus has its own big top tent. It has **theaters**. It has many different kinds of shows. The circus visits many cities each year.

Still, like long ago, everyone wants to watch the circus. Millions of people around the world see the shows each year. Why is that?

The Acts

No other circus is like Cirque du Soleil. Remember, there are no animals. Only people perform. And they are always surprising their audience. They think of new and **daring** things to do. They try things no one has tried before.

Vo·cab·u·lar·y

acts (akts)—different parts of shows people perform at the circus

stilts—high poles that people use to walk above the ground

theaters (thee•uh•tuhrz)—buildings where people put on a show

daring (dair•ing)—showing no fear; brave

The performers put on a spectacular show.

Acrobats

One show is performed all underwater. The audience watches from above. Another show starts with a surprise. A Japanese drummer plays Taiko (fat drum) drums—in the air. Strong wires connect him to the high **ceiling**. They hold him up. They hold his drums up. The wires are hidden. The drummer and his drums seem to float. The music makes your heart pound.

In many circuses, acrobats spin on ropes. In this circus, they use long cloth. They twist and turn from high above the audience. They hold onto the cloth. Sometimes they hold just with their legs. Black curtains hang behind the acrobats. The stage is black in back. **Spotlights** shine on the cloth. They light the acrobats. The acrobats dance in the air with the cloth. The shapes the acrobats make with their bodies and cloth keep changing. The act **thrills** everyone.

Acrobats wrap cloth around their bodies to stay steady.

Clarify Understanding by using photographs, charts, and other graphics to help me understand what I'm reading.

My Thinking
Wow—I can see in this photograph that the acrobats really do spin and twist on cloths. I think that looks like fun. I bet it is hard work!

Vo•cab•u•lar•y

ceiling (**see**•ling)—the inside upper surface of a room

spotlights (**spot**•lyts)—bright lights

thrills (thrilz)—excites; brings joy

Strategy

Clarify Understanding by using photographs, charts, and other graphics to help me understand what I'm reading.

My Thinking
I wonder what character this clown is playing? This looks like a very funny clown.

Clowns

The clowns in this circus look different from other clowns. The clowns fit the story of each show. They are **characters** in a story. Clowns **mime**. People laugh at the things clowns do.

One clown holds a garden hose. It leaks water. He talks to another clown and forgets about the hose. He lets water spray everywhere—even into the audience.

Suddenly the clown sees this. He looks shocked and sorry. Water soaks people who are watching. People laugh and clap wildly. This circus makes people happy, even if they leave dripping wet.

Clowns make funny faces.

The Studio in Montreal

Imagine going to a circus school. In the morning, you study math and reading. In the afternoon, you practice your clown tricks. You juggle balls. You can stand on a bicycle then flip over! You stand and ride and flip over.

In the evening, the circus performs. You are part of the show. People watch you juggle and ride the bike. They say, "o-o-o-h!" They say, "a-a-a-h!" You amaze them.

Now, imagine all your friends at this school. They are from all over the world. Some fold their bodies. Others walk the **tightrope** and still others swing on a **trapeze**. These are some things people learn to do at The Studio.

The Studio is the home of Cirque du Soleil. It is an enormous and beautiful building. It is in Montreal, Canada. Some people go there hoping to join the circus. They try out. They show their acts.

The circus always looks for new acts. They travel around the world looking for new acts. They find good acrobats and unusual clowns. They find gifted dancers.

When people are chosen to be performers, they go to The Studio.

Vo·cab·u·lar·y

characters (**kar**•uhk•tuhrz)—people in a story, book, play, or movie

mime (mym)—act out something without using words

tightrope (**tyt**•rohp)—a rope or wire stretched high above the ground

trapeze (tra•**peez**)—short bars hung from ropes and used by acrobats

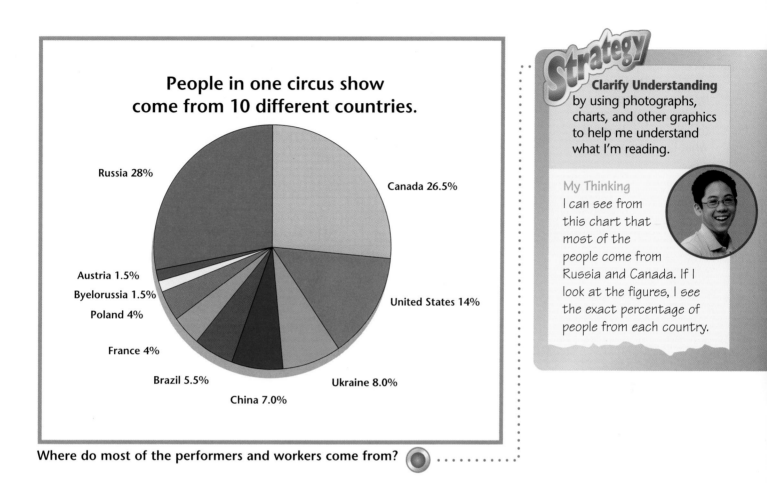

People in one circus show come from 10 different countries.

Russia 28%

Canada 26.5%

Austria 1.5%

Byelorussia 1.5%

Poland 4%

France 4%

United States 14%

Brazil 5.5%

Ukraine 8.0%

China 7.0%

Where do most of the performers and workers come from?

Strategy

Clarify Understanding by using photographs, charts, and other graphics to help me understand what I'm reading.

My Thinking
I can see from this chart that most of the people come from Russia and Canada. If I look at the figures, I see the exact percentage of people from each country.

Keeping It Safe

Everyone at the circus practices and practices. People love the work. But it is dangerous. They have to stay safe. To stay safe, they work with special equipment.

Soft plastic cubes cover the floor. If acrobats fall, they fall on soft cubes.

A **trampoline** covers part of the floor. It is fun to jump and bounce on, and it keeps people safe. Performers wear safety belts for work in the air. Nets catch people. Doctors are at every show to treat any injuries.

Behind the Scenes

Performers make up only a small part of the circus. Most people work behind the **scenes**. They are a big part of the show. But we do not see them. Hundreds of performers work for Cirque du Soleil. More than 1,000 people work behind the scenes.

Vo·cab·u·lar·y

trampoline (**tram**•puh•leen) —a sheet of canvas fastened with springs inside a metal frame; used for jumping and tumbling

scenes (seenz)—places where the actions or events occur

Strategy

Clarify Understanding
by using photographs, charts, and other graphics to help me understand what I'm reading.

My Thinking
I didn't realize how many jobs are behind the scenes of performances. I can see it would take many people to put on a show. The jobs seem very interesting. Maybe I'll be a director or lighting designer one day.

The Backstage Jobs

director	The *director* turns the idea for a show into a full circus performance.
choreographer	The *choreographer* creates and directs the movement of each performer.
composer	The *composer* creates the music for each show.
set designer	The *set designer* creates the look of the stage.
lighting designer	The *lighting designer* is in charge of the lights.
props team	The *props team* makes the things people use on-stage.
tech crew	The *tech crew* makes the floors and ceilings of the stage, and all of the equipment.
costume designer	The *costume designer* decides what each performer wears.

Cirque du Soleil is an unusual place to work. People in the offices at The Studio look out the window. They can see the artists rehearse. They see acrobats fly past. They see them swing on the trapeze. After work people can take lessons in circus **skills**. They can swing on a trapeze just for fun.

Giving and Teaching

Beautiful flower gardens are planted at The Studio. There are vegetable gardens, too. The circus uses the vegetables to feed the circus workers. Any extra food is given to people who live nearby.

This circus wants kids from all around the world to have fun. It wants kids to learn. The circus gives classes in many countries around the world. This way, many kids can learn circus skills. They learn to clown and juggle. They learn to flip, fold their bodies, and swing upside-down. In many places, there is no charge for the classes.

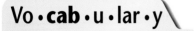

Vo·cab·u·lar·y

skills (skilz)—things you need to learn to do something well

Circus of Dreams Comes True

Cirque du Soleil started with a dream. Today, it is a dream come true. This circus wants to inspire everyone. Hold onto your dreams, they say. Your dreams can come true, too.

Another amazing performance by Cirque du Soleil

Think About
the
Strategy

AFTER READING

Respond
by drawing logical conclusions about the topic.

My Thinking
The strategy says to respond by drawing logical conclusions about the topic. Now that I've read this article, I know many things. And I can figure out even more. I think that the people who perform in Cirque du Soleil are athletic. (They work out so much.) I think they take good care of their bodies. (They eat healthful food.) I also think that all who work there— even those behind the scenes—enjoy their work. (It's rewarding to hear applause.)

Graphic organizers help us organize information we read. I think this text can be organized by using a comparison chart. A comparison chart compares one thing to another thing. I am going to compare Cirque du Soleil to other circuses. Here is how I organized the information. In the left-hand column, I listed four topics. Under "Cirque du Soleil" and "Other Circuses" I added facts and information about those topics.

Comparison Chart

The Wonders of Cirque du Soleil

	Cirque du Soleil	Other Circuses
Types of acts	• no animals • clowns • many acrobats • drummers	• animals • clowns • some acrobats • no drummers
Locations	• big top tents • theaters • underwater stages	• big top tents
Acrobats	• acrobats spin on red cloths • acrobats make shapes with bodies • many different kinds of shows	• acrobats spin on ropes • shows similar to each other
Clowns	• clowns are characters • fit the story of that show	• clowns the same from show to show

I used my graphic organizer to write a summary. Can you find the information in my summary that came from my comparison chart?

A Summary of
The Wonders of Cirque du Soleil

Cirque du Soleil is an unusual kind of circus. It is similar to other circuses in some ways, but is different in others. I will compare the types of acts, locations, acrobats, and clowns of Cirque du Soleil with those of other circuses.

Most circuses have animals, acrobats, and clowns in their shows. But, Cirque du Soleil has no animals at all. Cirque du Soleil has only people. Cirque du Soleil is different because its many acrobats move in unusual ways. They try daring things. They bend their bodies in odd ways. Cirque du Soleil also has drummers who perform in the air.

Both circuses and Cirque du Soleil use big top tents. But, Cirque du Soleil also has theaters. Some stages are even underwater.

In most circuses, acrobats spin on ropes. Cirque du Soleil is different. The acrobats spin on long cloths. They twist and turn from high above the audience. They hold onto the cloths. Sometimes they hold just with their legs. Acrobats dance in the air with the cloths. The shapes the acrobats make with their bodies and cloths keep changing. The acrobats put on many different types of shows.

The clowns in Cirque du Soleil look different from other clowns. In both circuses, the clowns mime. But, in Cirque du Soleil they are also characters in a story.

When you go to Cirque du Soleil, you see unusual acts and many different shows, acrobats, and clowns. It is different from anything else you will ever see.

Introduction
Here is how I developed my introductory paragraph. It gives readers an idea of what they are about to read.

Body
I used information from the boxes in the comparison matrix in my body paragraphs. The first paragraph tells how only people perform in Cirque du Soleil. The second and third paragraphs tell about the buildings and the types of acts. The fourth paragraph of the body tells about the clowns.

Conclusion
I concluded my paper by summarizing the main ideas.

Word Origins

In a dictionary, you can learn the **origin** of an entry word. That means that in addition to the meaning of the word, the dictionary tells you what language the word came from. English words come from many languages, including Greek, Latin, and French. Often, the origin of a word is given as an abbreviation, such as G., L., or F. (G means Greek, L means Latin, and F means French.)

In "The Wonders of Cirque du Soleil," you read the word *acrobat*. In the dictionary you would see the origin of the word like this:

> fr G. *akrobatos*, walking on tiptoe

That means that acrobat comes from the Greek word *akrobatos*, which means "walking on tiptoe."

Read these other words from "The Wonders of Cirque du Soleil." What can you learn about the origin of each word?

1. *circus*, fr L. *circus*, ring

2. *audience*, fr L. *audientia*, hear

3. *mime*, fr G. *mimos*, actor

4. *act*, fr L. *actus*, do

5. *cubes*, fr G. *kybos*, cube

Look up each word in a dictionary. On your own sheet of paper, write the origin of the word. (Hint: Some of these words may have two origins, for example, Latin and Greek.)

1. stage	**6.** current
2. nature	**7.** studio
3. palm	**8.** merchant
4. nasal	**9.** plastic
5. theater	**10.** scene

Readers' Theater

Work in a small group to read the following dialogue. The family in this dialogue has just been to see Cirque du Soleil. Practice reading, and when you're ready, perform it for your class.

Fluency TIP

As you practice reading this script, reflect the excitement and wonder in Laura and Tom's voices.

Narrator: Laura and Tom just saw a performance of Cirque du Soleil with their parents. After the show, they all talk about what they saw.

Laura: How did that woman walk on those high stilts? Why didn't she fall off? I couldn't do that!

Tom: And how could that man bend backward and poke his face between his ankles? And then he walked around the stage on his toes and palms, like a spider!

Mom: Those people are great athletes. They're acrobats.

Dad: They can do things with their bodies that most people can't.

Tom: How do they do it?

Dad: They train hard to learn those skills. They practice for years.

Laura: I liked the theater. The stage was so big! There was always something to watch.

Tom: And the lights and music were awesome! I want to see it again.

Mom: What acts did you like best, Tom?

Tom: I liked the mime. And the people on the trapeze were amazing!

Laura: I liked it best when they walked on the tightrope.

Mom: Oh, that made me so nervous. I was afraid they would fall off. It was hard to watch!

Dad: All of them were so daring! It was a fantastic show.

Narrator: The family reaches the car. Tom and Laura fall asleep on the way home. But they dream of the thrills they saw at the Cirque du Soleil, the Circus of the Sun.

Think About the Strategies

BEFORE READING

Set a Purpose

by using the title and headings to write questions that I can answer while I am reading.

 Write notes on your own paper to tell how you used this strategy.

DURING READING

Clarify Understanding

by using photographs, charts, and other graphics to help me understand what I'm reading.

 When you come to a red button like this ⦿, write notes on your own paper to tell how you used this strategy.

Racing in the Ironman

The Ironman race is about to begin.

The Ironman

Imagine you are going to race. You are going to race with hundreds of people. These people will come from all over the world. The race is long, and it is difficult. Many people want to win, but most just want to finish. The race is the Ironman triathlon. You will have to swim, bicycle, and run. Are you ready?

Swimming

First, you will have to swim more than two miles. You feel nervous and tense. You stretch to loosen up. If your muscles are too tense, you will not perform well. You focus. BANG! The race begins. **Participants** jump in the water. The water is cool on your skin. You swim like a fish.

Vo·cab·u·lar·y

participants
(pahr·**tis**·uh·puhnts)—
people who join others in an activity

[95]

Strategy

Clarify Understanding by using photographs, charts, and other graphics to help me understand what I'm reading.

Write notes on your own paper to tell how you used this strategy.

For some, swimming is the hardest part.

You swim far and fast to reach the turn **buoy**. The turn buoy **indicates** the halfway point. After swimming back to the shore, you will have completed the distance 2.4 miles.

Cycling

When you reach the shore, many other competitors are already there. However, the race is not over yet. Now, you have to ride 112 miles on your bike. You will have to save your **energy** by **pacing** yourself. You may have a small cramp in your leg from swimming. After you stretch your leg, you will feel better. You change from your swimsuit, and volunteers help you onto your bike.

Vo·cab·u·lar·y

buoy (**boo**•ee)—a floating object that is anchored in the water to warn of danger or to serve as a marker

indicates (**in**•di•kayts)—shows something

energy (**en**•uhr•jee)—strength

pacing (**pays**•ing)—to move at a steady rate of speed

Bicycling 112 miles is a challenge.

It is hot! The heat of the sun burns your shoulders. You are thirsty. You're tired and want to stop. Crowds of people stand along the side of the road. They cheer as you ride past. They give you **confidence** to ride on.

Running

Now it is time to put on your sneakers. You have to run 26.2 miles to finish. Your heart pumps. Your muscles throb. You breathe hard and your belly hurts. You want to quit. But after coming this far, you must go on. As you run, you **concentrate**. Your body wants to give up, but you are **determined**. You are nearing the finish line now. Your legs feel like jelly and your knees are wobbling. You can barely stay on your feet. Your head spins. You can hear the crowds cheering as you cross the finish line. Cameras flash! You are not first, but you have finished one of the hardest races in the world, the Ironman!

Running 26.2 miles is the last leg of the race.

Vo•cab•u•lar•y

confidence (**kon**•fi•duhns)— a strong feeling of faith and trust

concentrate (**kon**•suhn•trayt) —to keep one's thoughts, attention, or efforts focused on something

determined (di•**tur**•mind) —to make a firm choice

Strategy

Clarify Understanding by using photographs, charts, and other graphics to help me understand what I'm reading.

Write notes on your own paper to tell how you used this strategy.

Racers must be determined to reach the finish line.

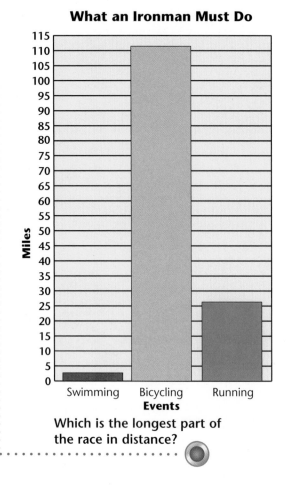

What an Ironman Must Do

Miles

Swimming   Bicycling   Running

Events

Which is the longest part of the race in distance?

What Is the Ironman?

The Ironman is a triathlon. A triathlon is an event based on three long-distance races: swimming, bicycling, and running. The Ironman is the hardest triathlon to finish because it is so long. Other triathlons have shorter distances.

Many Ironman races are held all over the world. The most important one is held in Hawaii. In 1978, John Collins, a navy officer, held the first Ironman in Hawaii. He wanted to see if anyone would go the distance with him. Fifteen people showed up. Twelve of them managed to finish. When other people heard about the race, they wanted to compete. The race has been held once a year ever since.

The People

The Ironman is not just for the **professional** athlete. Men and women, young and old, come from all over the world to race in Hawaii. Frank Day, one of the 12 people who finished the first Ironman, plans to race again. He is now almost 60 years old. He has been retired for nearly 10 years.

Not everyone who shows up has to race. A lot of people come just to watch. They crowd around to see the race. The crowds cheer the participants on. The athletes need **encouragement** because the race is hard. Nobody wants them to give up.

Training for the race

The Training

As in other sports, men and women must train for the Ironman. Athletes must run, swim, and cycle thousands of miles before they are ready. Being in shape is important. But just as important is to concentrate. Good concentration skills are difficult to maintain. If you are going to train, you must wake up early in the morning. You also have to eat well. Eating right makes a person strong. After you eat, you stretch. Your muscles must be loose. Then you jump into the pool and swim many laps. Next, you ride your bike for many miles. You can't rest for long because you still have to go running. Then you stretch again. Training requires dedication, concentration, and time.

Many athletes train in the mountains. The air is thinner there, and their lungs get strong from breathing the thin air. It is good to work out in many different **environments**. It is hot in Hawaii, so athletes must get used to the heat before racing. A person can get sick if he or she races and is not used to the heat.

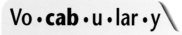

Vo•cab•u•lar•y

professional
(pruh•**fesh**•uh•nuhl)—a person who makes money for doing something

encouragement
(en•**kur**•ij•muhnt)—to give confidence by praising someone

environments
(en•**vy**•ruhn•muhnts)— the natural worlds of land, sea, and air

Strategy

Clarify Understanding by using photographs, charts, and other graphics to help me understand what I'm reading.

Write notes on your own paper to tell how you used this strategy.

Ironman Qualifying Races

Qualifying for the Ironman

In order to compete in the Ironman in Kona, Hawaii, athletes must first qualify. This means they must compete in other races and finish in a certain amount of time. In 2004, racers could choose from 25 races all over the world. Here are some of the places you could go to compete in an Ironman qualifying race.

United States	Worldwide	
Wisconsin	England	Brazil
Florida	Malaysia	France
California	New Zealand	Austria
St. Croix, U.S. Virgin Islands	South Africa	Germany
Maryland	Australia	Switzerland
Texas	Spain	Canada
Idaho	Japan	Korea
New York		

Family, Friends, and Teammates

An athlete needs family support. Ironman participant Cameron Brown says his family is his secret. His family helps him chase his dream. Andrea Fisher says that when she loses heart, her coach is caring. It is important to be happy. A person who is depressed gives up more easily.

Some athletes find it easier to train in a group. When athletes are feeling tired, the others help them continue. Training in a group also gives athletes new friends. It gives them support. And, sometimes it's just fun to train with other people around.

Why Do They Do It?

People like **challenges**. They do it to prove to themselves that it can be done. Some people hope to gain fame. Most people just hope to finish. People want to test their limits. One way is to beat records that have been set. Records, in this case, are the fastest times. The first record

Vo·cab·u·lar·y

challenges (**chal**•uhnj•es)— difficult things to do

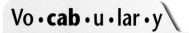

to beat was under 12 hours. That time was held by Gordon Haller. He was one of the 12 who ran the first race. The times have gotten harder to beat since. The fastest times now are under 9 hours. But the fastest times are beaten with every new race.

Many participants race only against their own times. They know they can't break records. But maybe they can **improve** and beat their own. This is called a Personal Record (PR). It is quite an **accomplishment** to set a new PR.

Summary

What is the Ironman race? It is a three-part competition in which athletes show one special trait—determination.

Vo·cab·u·lar·y

improve (im•**proov**)—
to make or become better

accomplishment
(uh•**kom**•plish•muhnt)—
a skill gained through training
and practice

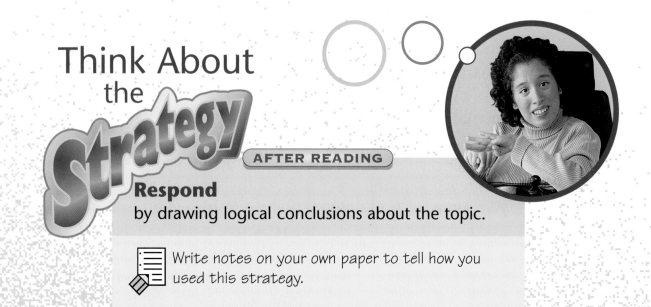

Think About the Strategy

AFTER READING

Respond
by drawing logical conclusions about the topic.

Write notes on your own paper to tell how you used this strategy.

Vocabulary

Prefixes for Numbers

A **prefix** gives a clue to a word's meaning. When you come across a word with a prefix whose meaning you know, use the prefix to figure out the meaning of the word. Some prefixes identify a number. For example,

uni—means one

bi—means two

tri—means three

quart—means four

penta—means five

In "Racing in the Ironman," the article refers to a sport called a *triathlon*. The prefix *tri-* means *three*, so we know that the sport refers to an event with three parts.

Following are other sports words with prefixes that are related to numbers.

unicycle—a vehicle with one wheel

bicycle—a vehicle with two wheels

tricycle—a vehicle with three wheels

quarter—one of four parts, as in a period during a football or basketball game

pentathlon—a contest involving five events

On your own sheet of paper, match the funny made-up sport on the left with the description of the sport on the right. Use your knowledge of number prefixes to help you.

1. tricatalon   **a.** a relay race between teams of four horses

2. bifrogathon **b.** one dog runs cross country

3. pentamicealon **c.** three cats race to climb a tree

4. unidogathon **d.** two frogs race a course of lily pads

5. quarthorseathon **e.** five mice compete to solve a maze

Now use your imagination and your knowledge of some number prefixes to create some fun new sports yourself. Combine the prefixes *uni-, bi-, tri-, quart-,* and *pent-* with your favorite animal to create a new sport. Next to each word, write a description of the event.

Monologue

A **monologue** is a long speech given by one person. You have read an article about the Ironman triathlon. Following is a monologue given by an Ironman athlete. Practice reading it aloud. Then read it aloud to the class with expression.

Fluency

TIP

As you practice, use your voice to express the various feelings of the athlete. Pause briefly between each thought.

I'm standing at the starting line. I feel ready for my race. It would be great to win, but I'll be happy if I finish. I've got to do my best!

The water feels cold, but I'm pushing through it fast. This leg of the Ironman race is a little more than 2 miles. But I feel strong!

Mission accomplished! I reached the turn buoy. Now I just have to swim back to shore.

Here I am, back on dry land. One leg down, 2 more to go—biking and running.

The volunteers are great. They have everything ready for me. Every second counts. I'm changing my clothes fast. Now I'm climbing onto my bike.

Whew! It's early in the day, but it's already hot. I've practiced many hours in weather like this, though. I know I can do it. I'm determined!

Look at the crowds on the sides of the road! That woman and that man are holding out bottles of water. Got it! That guy is handing out energy bars. I'll grab one later when I start feeling tired. They help a lot.

Things are going well. I made it past the biking finish line in good time. Now I "just" have to run 26.2 miles!

I'm lacing up my sneakers to start running the marathon. I do not have as much energy as I had before. I must concentrate on the job at hand. I want to finish!

Just a few miles to go! Wait! I've got to stop again to stretch my muscles because of cramps. I'm really tired now. Sweat is pouring down my body. Thanks to that lady along the road for pouring water over me. It feels good, and it keeps me cool.

Just a few more steps. I can do it!

It's been a great day. It's one of the best days of my life. I met the Ironman challenge.

Think About
the
Strategies

BEFORE READING

Set a Purpose
by using the title and headings to write questions that I can answer while I am reading.

DURING READING

Clarify Understanding
by using photographs, charts, and other graphics to help me understand what I'm reading.

AFTER READING

Respond
by drawing logical conclusions about the topic.

 Use your own paper to jot notes to apply these Before, During, and After Strategies. In this selection, you will choose when to stop, think, and respond.

The Special Olympics

Meet the Experts

What are experts? Experts are people who have great skills or knowledge in special areas. **Athletes** are experts in sports. Some athletes **compete** in large events, such as the Special Olympics. The athletes in the Special Olympics participate in events such as gymnastics, track and field, swimming, basketball, and much more. Athletes have many sports to choose from.

Challenges

So what makes the Special Olympics different from the Olympics? The Special Olympics are for athletes with **mental disabilities**. People with mental disabilities face many challenges. People with mental disabilities are often seen as being unable to do certain tasks. This may not be true though. Learning new skills may be big challenges for

Vo•cab•u•lar•y

athletes (**ath•**leets)—people who are trained or good at sports or games that require strength, speed, and agility

compete (kuhm•**peet**)— to work hard against another or others to win something

mental (**men**•tl)—having to do with the mind

disabilities (dis•uh•**bil**•i•teez)—limitations on what people can do

them. They still can accomplish many tasks. They are able to reach goals. According to one Special Olympics athlete, "You have to just keep on trying and never give up!" The members of the Special Olympics teams are truly experts in their chosen sport. They train hard, compete with **pride,** earn medals, and make their families and friends very proud.

What Is the Special Olympics?

The Special Olympics provides year-round sports training and athletic competition for people with mental disabilities. Training and local competitions are held in over 150 countries. Athletes can go on to compete in national events and in the world games. Athletes come from all over the world. By participating in the games, they become stronger and more active. They become part of a team. They show their **courage.** They share their joy with the world.

How Did the Special Olympics Begin?

Dr. Frank Hayden came up with the idea to hold training programs for people with mental disabilities. He knew that through training all people could improve their fitness levels. He also believed this to be true for those with mental disabilities.

Racing for the finish line

Dr. Hayden performed tests. He proved that people with disabilities could do many sports. They would need to try harder, and they would need support to succeed. Yet, they could do it.

Dr. Hayden wanted to start a sports program for the mentally disabled. Soon, Eunice Shriver heard what Dr. Hayden was trying to do. She ran day camps for the mentally disabled in her home. She wanted to

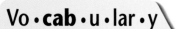

Vo•**cab**•u•lar•y

pride (preyed)—a sense of one's own worth; self-respect; pleasure or satisfaction in accomplishments

courage (**kur**•ij)—bravery; fearlessness

help Dr. Hayden start the program. With her help, the Special Olympic games started in 1968. People from around the world started taking part. By 2005, more than 2 million athletes will take part in the events.

Volunteers and Family

During the Special Olympics, **volunteers** come from all over to help. These are people who want to give their time and energy. Some volunteers work only a few hours during a race. Others volunteer for several hours nearly every week of the year.

Volunteers are of all ages. Some are high school students. Others are seniors who are retired. About 500,000 volunteers help out in all.

Many volunteers are from the same hometowns as the athletes. They believe in the athletes. The athletes need support to do their best. Everyone wants them to do their best. When they do, it is exciting. Everyone feels pride and joy.

The athletes' family members come to cheer them on. Mothers, fathers, sisters, brothers, aunts, and uncles come from all over the world to show their support. Sometimes it is hard for so many people from one family to make such a long **journey**. But it is important to the athletes. It is worth it.

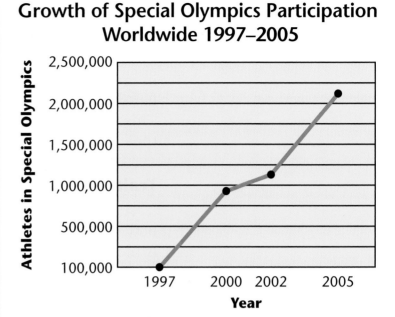

Growth of Special Olympics Participation Worldwide 1997–2005

The crowd cheers for the athletes.

Vo·cab·u·lar·y

volunteers (vol•uhn•**teerz**)—those who offer to do a job without getting paid

journey (**jur**•nee)—traveling from one place to another

Coaches

The athletes in the Special Olympics need coaches. Coaches play an important role in the event. Coaches do lots of things. They give the athletes the skills to compete in an event. They show the athlete how to do well in his or her sport. Coaches cheer on their athletes in many ways. This happens before the event. It happens during and after the event, as well. Coaches show the athlete how to grow.

Training

Athletes spend much time training. They train to learn new skills. They need to be brave to try new sports. Athletes who swim must be able to hold their breath underwater. This can be scary for someone who is trying this for the first time.

Coaches, volunteers, and family members all support the athletes as they train.

Athletes also learn how to work with others as a team. They learn to **cooperate** with their teammates. They learn to accept help from volunteers. Families and volunteers help with training. Volunteers who live in the same home-towns coach the athletes. Family members get to know the volunteers. The athletes, the volunteers, the coaches, and the family are all part of the team.

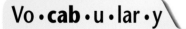

Vo·cab·u·lar·y

cooperate (koh•op•uh•rayt)— to work or act together for a common purpose

The Events

How many Special Olympics events are held around the world? Each year there are at least 20,000 competitions! Every day, people all over the world are training for an event. As athletes train, they can prepare for national and even world competitions. Someone might be learning swimming skills in France. Someone might be learning skating skills in Africa. In 2003, an event was held in Ireland. In 2005, one will be held in Japan. And, in 2006, an event will be held in Iowa in the United States.

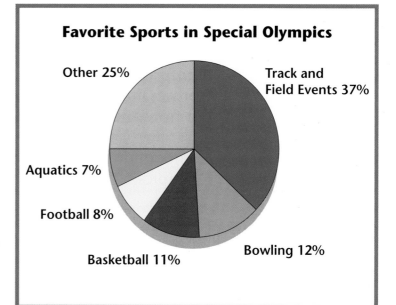

Favorite Sports in Special Olympics

Other 25%
Track and Field Events 37%
Aquatics 7%
Football 8%
Bowling 12%
Basketball 11%

"Other" sports include golf, table tennis, and sailing

The Sports

Athletes of all abilities and ages can compete. Athletes can choose from many different events. A runner can choose the long-distance race or the dash. There is also skiing and skating. Other sports are played with a team. Volleyball is played with teams. So is softball. The chart on this page shows the top five sports. Track and field events are the most popular.

Let Me Be Brave

The real reward of the Special Olympics is everyone's happiness. Success comes when the athletes do their best. They have overcome big challenges. They have learned to "go all the way" and not give up. In their hearts, they know the **oath** they have sworn. It says,

Let me win, but if I cannot win, let me be brave in my attempt!

Vo·cab·u·lar·y

oath (ohth)—a serious promise

Compound Words

A **compound word** is a word that is made up of two smaller words. Often, the meaning of the compound word can be figured out from the words that make it up.

Compound words related to sports appear in "The Special Olympics." Two compound words are *volleyball,* and *softball.*

Read these other sports-related compound words.

base + ball= baseball
foot + ball = football
play + back = playback
swim + suit = swimsuit
back + hand = backhand

Find pairs of words from the following list that make a compound word related to sports and games. Seven answers are possible. Write them on your own piece of paper.

surf   hand

  wind   ball   board

speed   snow

  way   dive   sky

Interview

You have read how special the Special Olympics really is. Read this interview between a reporter and a coach in the Special Olympics. Read the interview aloud with a classmate. Practice reading until you are comfortable with all of the words. Then read it aloud to the class.

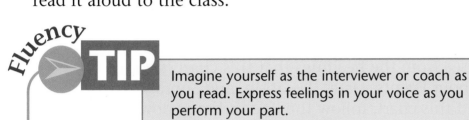

Fluency TIP

Imagine yourself as the interviewer or coach as you read. Express feelings in your voice as you perform your part.

Interviewer: Hello, Coach. Thanks for agreeing to this interview.

Coach: I would do anything for the Special Olympics News—anything for the kids.

Interviewer: Why did you become a Special Olympics coach?

Coach: I was a high school track coach. One of my students had a sister with mental disabilities. I learned about Special Olympics through their family. I decided to coach for Special Olympics as a way to help my student's sister and also to help our community.

Interviewer: What has been the most challenging part of coaching?

Coach: Well, I guess the most challenging part is training children and adults who have never trained before. For many, this is the first time they have been in a pool or on a track or played ball with a team.

Interviewer: Are the athletes scared?

Coach: Sure, I think some of them are. They are scared just like anybody is when they try something new. But you should see them once they have swum or run their first lap . . . or the first time they finish a ball game. They are very proud. I am very proud of them.

Interviewer: It seems like you should be proud of yourself.

Coach: I'm mostly proud of my athletes . . . and of all of the people who support them. There is nothing else in the world like seeing the smiling faces of these wonderful athletes as they cross their finish lines. It is one of the best jobs I have ever had!

Chart

Special Olympic Events

The following chart lists some of the upcoming events in the Special Olympics. Notice that the dates are on the left side of the chart. They go from 2005 to 2007. Look at the headings across the top of the chart. You see from the headings that this chart is going to give information about Events, Dates, Location, and Some Sports. When you read this chart, follow the line across or down to get the correct information. Use the chart to answer the questions on the next page. Be sure to read carefully.

Special Olympic Events Around the World

Year	Events	Dates	Location	Some Sports
2005	Special Olympics World Winter Games	February 26– March 5, 2005	Nagano, Japan	• Alpine skiing • cross-country skiing • figure skating • floor hockey • snowboarding • speed skating
2006	Special Olympics U.S. National Games	July 3–8, 2006	Iowa, USA	• aquatics • basketball • gymnastics • powerlifting • softball • track and field • volleyball
2007	Special Olympics World Summer Games	October 10–19, 2007	Shanghai, People's Republic of China	• bowling • cycling • golf • judo • sailing • soccer • table tennis

Discussion Questions

Answer these questions with a partner or on a separate piece of paper.

1. Which of these events occurs last according to this chart?
   a. Special Olympics U.S. National Games
   b. Special Olympics World Summer Games
   c. Special Olympics World Winter Games
   d. none of the above

2. During what season will the games in Shanghai, People's Republic of China be held?

3. If an athlete from the United States wants to compete in her own country, to which games would she go?

4. Why are events such as snowboarding usually held in the winter months?

5. If athletes want to compete when they are older, which games might they compete in?
   a. Special Olympics World Winter Games
   b. Special Olympics U.S. National Games
   c. Special Olympics World Summer Games
   d. Special Olympics National Summer Marathon

6. To which games will some athletes probably bring golf clubs?
   a. Special Olympics World Winter Games
   b. Special Olympics U.S. National Games
   c. Special Olympics World Summer Games
   d. Special Olympics Swimmer's Marathon

7. If a volunteer is working for the games held in Japan, what dates would he or she need to be in that country?
   a. July 3–8, 2006
   b. October 10–19, 2007
   c. January 4–9, 2004
   d. February 26–March 5, 2005

8. Which sport would a spectator most enjoy if he or she likes to see gymnasts?

CONNECTING
to the Real World

EXPLORE MORE

Make a Flip Book
On ten sheets of paper, draw an acrobat at different steps in doing a circus act. Staple the sheets together on the left side. Flip through them to see the acrobat moving.

Draw an Imaginary Person
Stretch the limits of what real people can do with their bodies. Think of unusual things the body parts can do. (Example: an arm that can extend several feet to reach things on high shelves) Draw a super-person and label its parts.

Create Sports or Fitness Awards
Create ribbons to be given as awards for kinds of fitness. Examples are: Fastest Walker, Best Basketball Player, and Most Improved Catcher. Present the awards at the end of the school year.

Set Goals
Think of something about your athletic ability that you would like to improve. This may be to run faster or longer or to do more jumping jacks. Keep a chart of your progress. See how you do at the end of one month.

Research a Special Olympics Sport
Use books or the Internet to find out more about a sport at the Special Olympics. Write a report and draw pictures to show what you learned. Post your report on a bulletin board.

Related Books

Brown, Fern G. *Special Olympics.* F. Watts, 1992.

Donkin, Andrew. *DK Readers: Going for Gold.* DK Publishing, 1999.

Harmer, Mabel. *Circus.* Scholastic, 1981.

Hayhurst, Chris. *ULTRA Marathon Running.* Rosen Publishing Group, 2002.

Jordan, Denise M. *Circus Performers.* Heinemann Library, 2002.

Kennedy, Mike. *Special Olympics.* Children's Press, 2003.

Knotts, Bob. *Summer Olympics.* Scholastic, 2000.

Lund, Bill. *Triathlon.* Capstone Press, 1996.

Oxlade, Chris, and David Ballheimer. *Eyewitness: Olympics.* DK Publishing, Inc., 2002.

Robertson, Patrisha Grainger. *Cirque du Soleil: A Parade of Colors.* Harry N. Abrams, 2003.

Scheppler, Bill. *The Ironman Triathlon.* Rosen Central, 2002.

Sports Illustrated for Kids Staff. *Sports Illustrated for Kids Year in Sports 2004.* Scholastic, 2004.

Interesting Web Sites

Check out the following Web sites for more information about topics in this unit.

Cirque du Soleil

www.cirquedusoleil.com/

Ironman

http://vnews.ironmanlive.com/

www.sikids.com

Special Olympics

www.specialolympics.org

www.cbvcp.com/specialolympics/

Web sites have been carefully researched for accuracy, content, and appropriateness. However, teachers and caregivers are reminded that Web sites are subject to change. Internet use should always be monitored.

Unit 4 Strategies

BEFORE READING

Preview the Selection

by looking at the photographs, illustrations, captions, and graphics to predict what the selection will be about.

DURING READING

Make Connections

by comparing my experiences with what I'm reading.

AFTER READING

Recall

by using the headings to question myself about what I read.

LEARN
the strategies
in the selection
John Muir: Protecting Our Lands
page 119

PRACTICE
the *strategies*
in the selection
Jacques Cousteau: Crusader of the Sea
page 131

APPLY
the *strategies*
in the selection
Mae C. Jemison: Soaring to the Sky
page 141

Think About the
Strategies

Preview the Selection

by looking at the photographs, illustrations, captions, and graphics to predict what the selection will be about.

My Thinking

The strategy says to look at the photographs, illustrations, captions, and graphics to predict what the selection will be about. I'll look at the pictures before I start to read. They will help me figure out what I'm about to read. Some of the photographs show John Muir at different points in his life. Some are of him at a mountainside. There's also a map with information about Yosemite National Park, along with statistics. I predict that the selection will be about Muir's life and what he did for Yosemite. I'll read on to see if I'm right.

DURING READING

Make Connections

by comparing my experiences with what I'm reading.

My Thinking

The strategy says to make connections by comparing my experiences with what I'm reading. This means I need to think about things that have happened in my own life. I will stop and think about this strategy every time I come to a red button like this ●.

JOHN MUIR: PROTECTING OUR LANDS

John Muir, man of the mountains

Have you seen the Grand Canyon? Have you camped in Yosemite? Have you gone swimming at Cape Cod National Seashore? All of these places are national parks.

If you have been to a national park, you have John Muir to thank. He helped build the whole national park system.

A Passion for the Wild

John Muir was born in 1838. He spent his first years in Scotland. His town was located on the North Sea coast. There the weather can be fierce. But there were wild places to **explore**.

> **Vo•cab•u•lar•y**
>
> **explore** (ik•**splor**)—to find and learn about new places or things

Strategy

Make Connections by comparing my experiences with what I'm reading.

My Thinking
I like to observe nature, too. I look at the trees and flowers on my way to and from school.

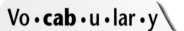

The youngster felt a strong tie to nature. Nature was a **passion** for John. It was an emotional bond. This bond would shape his life.

When John was 11 years old, the Muir family moved to the United States. They farmed in Wisconsin. The boy worked hard. He dug wells. He plowed the soil. And he got to know the deep woods.

John did not have much time for school. But he hungered for knowledge. He read. He observed nature.

He also was an **inventor**. He was good at thinking up new ways to make things work. One day, the University of Wisconsin asked him to study there.

Sometime during college, though, the young man left. He was in his mid-twenties. It was time to explore the world.

Traveling Light

Muir set off on foot. He walked many miles west, sometimes finding jobs along the way. He went alone into the **wilderness** of Canada and the United States.

He liked to travel light. He carried only a few things. He would take just a blanket, some bread, and tea. He took just enough to take care of himself in the wild.

But Muir always took a notebook. He wrote about the beautiful things he saw. He drew pictures, too. You can feel the passion for nature in his work.

A statue of the young John Muir

Vo•cab•u•lar•y

passion (**pash**•uhn)—
a strong feeling for something

inventor (in•**ven**•tuhr)—
someone who thinks up and makes new things

wilderness (**wil**•duhr•nis)—
a wild, natural area; undisturbed by humans

After a few years, Muir went to California. He arrived in the big city of San Francisco. He asked how to get to the wilderness. He was told to head toward the mountains. Muir took the advice. Again, he walked.

To the Mountains

Muir reached Yosemite [yoh•**sem**•i•tee] Valley. It is a big, wild place. It is in a mountain range called the Sierra Nevadas. The beauty of the Sierras thrilled Muir.

Yosemite Valley is an amazing place. Rock cliffs soar into the sky. Waterfalls thread down their sides. Many plants and animals live there. There are countless meadows, lakes, and trees. There are groves of giant trees called **sequoias**. Some are more than 3,000 years old!

For a while, Muir worked on a ranch in the valley. He herded sheep. He worked at a sawmill, too. At a sawmill, trees are cut up to make paper and build houses.

But Muir found trouble in the mountains. What problems did Muir find?

Strategy

Make Connections by comparing my experiences with what I'm reading.

My Thinking
I saw giant sequoias on a nature show on television once. They can be as tall as 100 to 385 feet. The trunk of the tree can be up to 25 feet in diameter. They are huge trees!

Muir was happiest when walking and climbing in Yosemite.

Vo•cab•u•lar•y

sequoias (si•**kwoy**•uhz)— large evergreen trees that have reddish wood

[121]

Strategy

Make Connections
by comparing my experiences with what I'm reading.

My Thinking
I know about writing articles for magazines. An article of mine was printed in the school magazine. My friends and family read it.

Nature in Peril

Muir saw that ranching hurt the **environment**. Sheep and cattle damaged the land.

Logging was a big problem, too. Logging companies cut down many trees. They were **destroying** land and hurting wildlife.

Logging must be done carefully and in the right way in order to protect the environment.

The ranchers and loggers just wanted to make money. They did not care about the mountains and forests. They were even cutting down the ancient sequoias!

At that time, many people thought they should **tame** nature. They thought humans could use everything on Earth. They did not care if they harmed the environment.

Muir felt differently. He thought wild places should be left alone. He thought people should protect nature, not harm it. He believed in **conservation**.

Could he help save these special places?

Taking Action

Muir decided he must tell people about nature. He wrote articles. They were printed in magazines.

Vo•**cab**•u•lar•y

environment (en•**vy**•ruhn•muhnt)—all the things in the natural world, including rocks, soil, air, water, and living things

destroying (di•**stroy**•ing)— ruining

tame—to control

conservation (kon•sur•**vay**•shuhn)— protecting nature

Readers could feel his passion in the words. Muir helped them see nature differently. He urged readers to visit the wilderness. He told them they would find peace and comfort there. He wrote, "Going to the mountains is going home."

Muir changed how people thought. They saw things in a new light. They saw that humans should not try to tame nature. They should find ways to live in **harmony** with the environment. They had to set limits on how nature was used. If they did not, beautiful places and wild things would be lost forever. It was the start of the conservation movement.

The Movement Grows

Muir traveled the world to spread his message. He explored other wild places. He wrote and wrote.

He became famous. People read his words. They saw pictures of him. They heard him talk. He was gentle. He had a kind face. People felt at ease with him. They trusted what he had to say.

Muir brought people who care about conservation together. They formed a club called the Sierra Club. The people in this club protect and preserve the national parks and forests. You may have heard of it. The Sierra Club is still going strong today.

Important people got in touch with Muir. They had **influence**. They could help decide how nature could be used. They could set good limits.

In the early 1900s, Muir worked with President Theodore Roosevelt. They talked about conservation.

Strategy

Make Connections by comparing my experiences with what I'm reading.

My Thinking
I have heard of the Sierra Club. My parents are members. I've joined in on some of the youth activities.

Muir (right) worked with President Theodore Roosevelt to set up more national parks.

Vo·cab·u·lar·y

harmony (har•muh•nee)— being comfortable together; equal

influence (in•floo•uhns)— the power or ability to decide how things are done

Strategy

Make Connections by comparing my experiences with what I'm reading.

My Thinking
I know about enjoying historical sites. I've been to the Statue of Liberty and it's awesome! I've also been to some of the national parks. I'm glad John Muir was able to protect these special places.

President Roosevelt and Muir made plans to protect more wild places forever. They wanted to set up more national parks. National parks are areas that are kept in their natural state by the government. These areas are protected. Thanks to their work, Yosemite was made a national park in 1890. Muir also helped create other national parks, like Grand Canyon National Park. President Roosevelt became known as the "conservation president." He doubled the number of national parks. The sequoias were saved, too.

Today, hundreds of wild areas are protected as national parks. Historical sites are protected, too, like the Statue of Liberty. Even some special roads are part of the national park system. Millions of people enjoy these places every year.

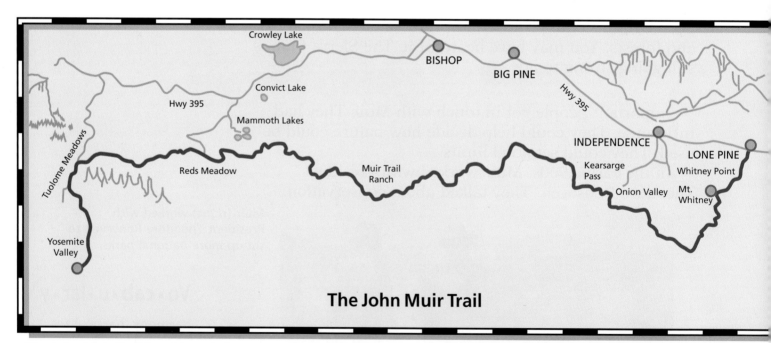

The John Muir Trail

The John Muir Trail is a 211 mile long hiking and backpacking trail in California. Named after John Muir, this trail passed through 14,000 foot peaks, lakes, canyons, and cliffs. The trail runs through three National Parks: Yosemite, Kings Canyon, and Sequoia.

John Muir—Nature's Hero

John Muir died in 1914 at the age of 76. Today he is known as the "father of our national parks." Thanks in great part to his efforts, special wild places still exist. We can still find peace and comfort there. We can still walk among the soaring cliffs and waterfalls of Yosemite Valley. Thanks to Muir, sequoias still shade the earth.

Think About the Strategy

AFTER READING

Recall
by using the headings to question myself about what I read.

My Thinking

The strategy says I should recall by using the headings to question myself about what I read. I reread each heading and then thought about what I learned.

The first heading is "A Passion for the Wild." Now I know that Muir was passionate about the nature around him. With the next heading, "Traveling Light," I remember that Muir carried few things as he traveled through the wilderness of the United States and Canada. In "To the Mountains," Muir was thrilled with the beauty of the Sierras and with Yosemite Valley. In "Nature in Peril," Muir disliked the way the land was being abused. He believed it should be conserved. In "Taking Action," he wrote articles about how people should treat nature with care. "The Movement Grows" shows how the conservation movement and the Sierra Club have grown.

"John Muir—Nature's Hero" summarizes what an important person John Muir was. His efforts still affect all of us today. We have him to thank for our beautiful national parks.

Graphic organizers help us organize information we read. I think this article can be organized by using a web. I put the title of the article I read in the middle circle. Then, I put details about the article on the arms.

Web

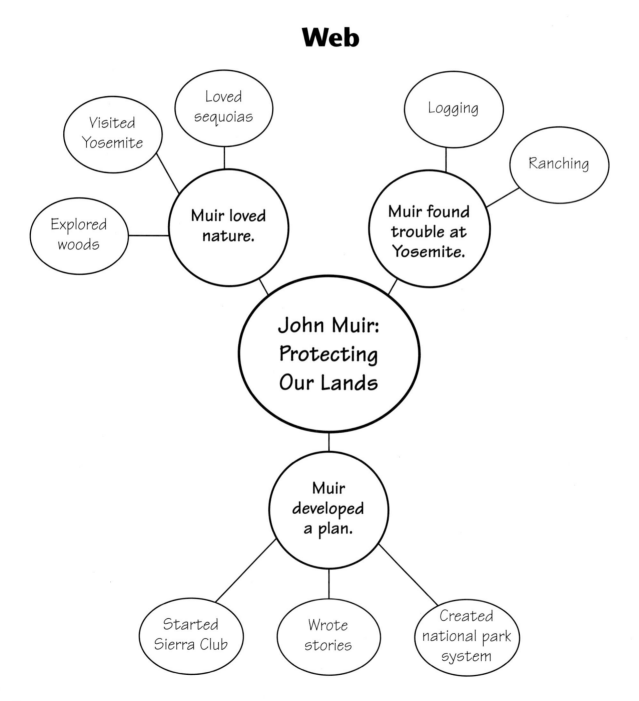

I used my graphic organizer to write a summary of the article. Can you find the information in my summary that came from my web?

A Summary of
John Muir: Protecting Our Lands

John Muir loved nature even as a little boy. He was passionate about nature. He wanted to spend time working in nature and saving the wilderness.

John Muir was born in 1838. As a child, he loved to explore the wild woods. He loved to observe nature. As a young adult, he visited Yosemite Valley in California. He loved the big sequoia trees that grew there. He loved exploring everything wild.

While at Yosemite Valley, Muir saw some troublesome things. He saw that ranchers and loggers harmed the land and the trees. Muir wanted all people to love and protect nature from harm. He was worried about the environment's future.

John Muir developed a plan to save the nature he loved. He wrote stories about it. He talked to people about how to protect nature. Part of Muir's plan was to protect Yosemite. He created the national park system. He made Yosemite the first national park in the system. He also started the Sierra Club.

Was John Muir's plan successful? Yes! Today, the national park system protects hundreds of wild areas from harm. The sequoia trees are safe. The land is safe. Every year, millions of people visit these wild places. Muir's love of nature made a difference. Although he died in 1914, Muir's efforts can still be felt. He started the conservation movement that is active to this day.

Introduction
My introductory paragraph tells readers what they are about to read. You can find this information in the center of my web.

Body
I used information from my web for each paragraph in the body of my paper. One paragraph tells about Muir's love of nature. Another tells about the trouble he found at Yosemite. The third paragraph tells about his plans. Then, I developed each idea by adding details.

Conclusion
I summarized my paper by recalling the main ideas.

Prefixes

A **prefix** is a word part placed at the beginning of a word. A prefix affects the meaning of a word. It can give you a good clue about a word's meaning.

The prefix *ex-* comes from Greek and means "out of" or "from." The word *exhale,* for example, means "to breathe out."

You read the following sentence in *John Muir: Protecting Our Land:*

> It was time to **explore** the world.

The word *explore* means "to go out and travel for the purpose of discovery."

Look at these words that begin with *ex-.* Look at their meanings. Think about how *ex-* is part of the meaning.

Word	Meaning
extend	to reach out
extract	to pull out
extinct	died out
export	to send out
excavate	to dig out

Read each sentence. Find a word from the word column above that makes sense in the sentence. Words may be used more than once. Write your answer on your own piece of paper.

1. The machine can _____ water from the wet cloth.

2. Dinosaurs have been _____ for millions of years.

3. Let's _____ the new pencils to China.

4. Please _____ your hand to reach the ceiling.

5. Archaeologists _____ fossils.

6. When we exercise, we _____ our arms and legs.

7. The dentist must _____ the bad tooth.

8. The group is working to save the chimpanzees so they will not become _____ .

Essay

Read this essay written by a student. Practice it by yourself. Then read it out loud with expression to a partner.

Fluency

TIP

Be sure to read this essay in a loud, clear voice. Think about your audience and how the essay will sound to them.

My Hero, John Muir

There are many people in my life who are special. One of the people I most admire is John Muir. He lived almost a century ago. But, because of him, I can go to places like Yosemite and the Grand Canyon. They are national parks. They are filled with nature.

Muir knew that these were special places. Back in his day, he saw that something had to be done to keep the loggers and ranchers from destroying land. He even worked with President Theodore Roosevelt to find ways to protect the special places. They worked together to create the national park system! Mr. Muir also started the Sierra Club. It is one of the most important conservation groups. Today, it has about 70,000 members! My parents and I belong to the Sierra Club. It feels good to be part of it.

When Muir was a young man, he went into the woods. He always took a notebook. He drew pictures of the beautiful things he saw. He wrote about them, too. People read his articles. They said they could feel his passion for nature in his work. Once he wrote, "Going to the mountains is going home." That helped start the conservation movement.

I think Mr. Muir would be happy to know that I care about the environment, just like he did.

Think About the

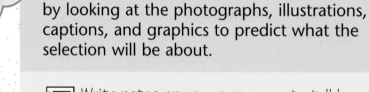

BEFORE READING

Preview the Selection

by looking at the photographs, illustrations, captions, and graphics to predict what the selection will be about.

 Write notes on your own paper to tell how you used this strategy.

DURING READING

Make Connections

by comparing my experiences with what I'm reading.

When you come to a red button like this ⦿, write notes on your own paper to tell how you used this strategy.

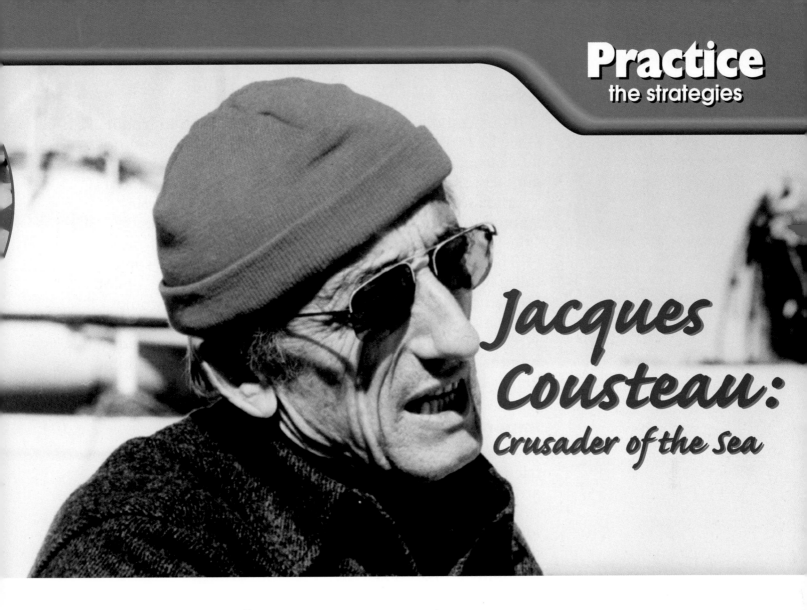

Jacques Cousteau: Crusader of the Sea

The Day It Started

The year was 1936. A young man named Jacques was diving in the ocean. He was with friends. For fun, he dove under the water. He wore **goggles**. He was **amazed** at the things he could see! He wanted other people to see them, too.

And he did. After that, Jacques Cousteau [koo•stoh] studied undersea life. He helped people see the world under the sea.

Early Loves

Cousteau was born in France. The year was 1910. He always loved the water. He learned to swim when he was 4 years old.

Cousteau also loved making movies. At 13, he bought a small movie camera. He wanted to see how it worked. So, he took it apart. Then he put it back together. He started making movies.

Vo•cab•u•lar•y

goggles (gog•uhlz)—special protective glasses that fit tightly around your eyes

amazed (uh•mayzd)— surprised

[131]

Strategy

Make Connections by comparing my experiences with what I'm reading.

Write notes on your own paper to tell how you used this strategy.

Vo·cab·u·lar·y

rules (roolz)—official orders that tell you what to do

accident (**ak**•si•duhnt)— an event that takes place unexpectedly and that often involves damage

exercised (**ek**•suhr•syzd)— made your body work hard repeatedly in order to get or stay healthy

strapped (strapt)—to be held together with a belt, cable, or rope

mouthpiece (**mowth**•pees) —the piece of an instrument that goes in the mouth

School

Cousteau did not love school. He was often in trouble. Once he broke 17 windows in school. The school did not let Cousteau back inside. Then his parents sent him to another school. It had many **rules**. The boy did well there.

After school, Cousteau joined the French navy. He wanted to travel. He wanted to work on the ocean. Cousteau trained on a ship. It sailed around the world.

Then Cousteau decided to be a navy pilot. But something bad happened. It was just before he became a pilot. He had a bad car **accident**. The doctors said he would never move his arms again.

Cousteau did not believe the doctors. He **exercised** for months. Finally, he could use both arms. But he could no longer be a pilot.

Important Friends

Cousteau was getting better. Then, he made two new friends. One said that swimming would make Cousteau's arms stronger. It did.

All three friends loved the water. They would see how long they could stay underwater. They tried to see how deep they could dive. They tried to invent things that would help them dive.

The year was 1936. One day, the three friends were diving together. Cousteau wore his pilot's goggles. This changed his life. Cousteau could see clearly underwater! He said, "My eyes were opened on the sea."

Breathing Underwater

Divers used to wear thick, heavy suits. They had to be connected to a long air hose. Cousteau and another friend changed that. In 1943, they invented the scuba tank.

The tank is **strapped** to the diver's back. A short tube brings air from the tank to the diver's **mouthpiece**. The diver can move easily underwater. The diver can stay underwater for a long time.

The friends tested the new tank. They made hundreds of dives. As they dove deeper, they made another find.

Thanks to Cousteau's invention, thousands of people go scuba diving today.

Strategy

Make Connections by comparing my experiences with what I'm reading.

Write notes on your own paper to tell how you used this strategy.

They already knew about the air we breathe. It is mostly a gas called **nitrogen**. Something strange happened when the divers went more than 100 feet down. They found out that nitrogen could build up in their brains. When this happened, the divers got confused. They thought they did not need their scuba tanks anymore. They took them off. This could have turned out badly. Fortunately, everything turned out all right. They made it back to the surface unharmed. But the diving friends learned a valuable lesson.

The information they learned not only helped them, but it helped other divers, too. They learned to set limits on how deep to dive. They told other divers how long it was safe to stay underwater.

Cousteau even invented a special belt. It helped divers come out of the water when they were ready. It also helped keep them deep in the water for as long as they wanted to stay there.

Filming Underwater

Cousteau wanted to film the work they were doing. He wanted to make movies. But cameras did not work underwater at the time. He put a special **lens** on a movie camera. His friends helped. They put the camera in a box. The box was safe from water. How did they adjust the lens? They moved a clothespin that stuck out of the box.

Vo•cab•u•lar•y

nitrogen (ny•truh•juhn)— part of the air we breathe

lens (lenz)—a piece of glass or plastic that helps with focus

[133]

Cousteau bought many rolls of movie-camera film. But the rolls would have to be connected in order to work. This had to be done in a dark place. Cousteau worked under blankets at night to connect the rolls. Now, Cousteau could film what they saw underwater.

The *Calypso*

Cousteau became famous. He was an ocean explorer. In 1950, he bought his own ship. He named it *Calypso*.

Cousteau made changes to the ship. He had a diving hole cut into it. He added an underwater room. That helped him see out. The *Calypso* set sail in 1951. Cousteau hired **scientists** to go with him. Together, they explored the seas.

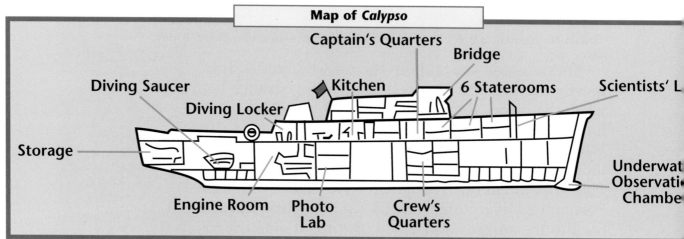

Map of *Calypso*

Diving Saucer · Diving Locker · Storage · Engine Room · Photo Lab · Crew's Quarters · Captain's Quarters · Kitchen · Bridge · 6 Staterooms · Scientists' L... · Underwat... Observati... Chambe...

By looking at the photo and the diagram, you can see what the *Calypso* was like inside and out.

Vo·cab·u·lar·y

scientists (sy•uhn•tists)—those who study nature and the physical world

The First Book

In 1953, Cousteau wrote his first book. He called it *The Silent World*. It had underwater photographs—in color. His book was printed in 22 languages. It sold millions of copies. He later made it into an award-winning documentary film.

Saucers and Laboratories

Cousteau still wanted to learn more about the ocean. During the 1950s, he built several diving **saucers**. They could dive very deep. Cousteau could film things never seen before.

In the 1960s, Cousteau had 3 underwater **laboratories** built. People lived in them. Some stayed for up to a month.

The Undersea World of Jacques Cousteau

In 1966, a television station asked Cousteau to make 12 shows. They were called *The Undersea World of Jacques Cousteau*. People saw all sorts of fish and animals. They saw

Strategy

Make Connections by comparing my experiences with what I'm reading.

Write notes on your own paper to tell how you used this strategy.

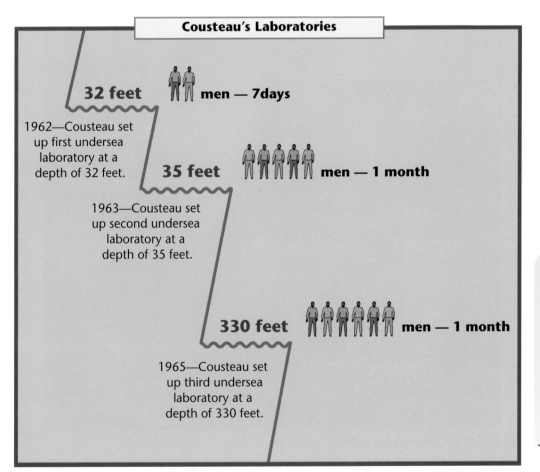

Cousteau's Laboratories

32 feet — men — 7days

1962—Cousteau set up first undersea laboratory at a depth of 32 feet.

35 feet — men — 1 month

1963—Cousteau set up second undersea laboratory at a depth of 35 feet.

330 feet — men — 1 month

1965—Cousteau set up third undersea laboratory at a depth of 330 feet.

Vo•**cab**•u•lar•y

saucers (**saw**•suhrz)—small, shallow, round, platelike objects

laboratories (**lab**•ruh•tor•eez) —rooms or buildings that contain special equipment for doing scientific tests, research, and experiments

[135]

eels, sharks, and snails. The plants and animals were beautiful colors. Most people were seeing these things for the first time.

Protecting the Oceans

Jacques Cousteau wanted to do more than study the ocean. He wanted to teach people about the oceans and ocean life. He also wanted to teach people how to protect our oceans and ocean life.

In 1973, Cousteau formed a new group. He named it the Cousteau Society. This society teaches people how to protect the earth in many ways. It reminds people to keep the ocean clean. It still does that today.

The Cousteau Society has developed special programs to teach students about the ocean. Students can go on sea cruises designed to teach them about the ocean and how to protect it. The society is also working to keep toxic substances from hurting the ocean and the life that inhabits it. This is just a short list of ways that the Cousteau Society is helping to protect our valuable oceans.

Cousteau was always curious about the sea.

Jacques Cousteau's Legacy

Jacques Cousteau died in 1997. He was 87 years old. His discoveries changed our world. He helped us see things in a new way. His work to teach about and protect our oceans and our Earth has made our world a better place. His work will continue through those who follow in his footsteps.

Strategy

Make Connections by comparing my experiences with what I'm reading.

Write notes on your own paper to tell how you used this strategy.

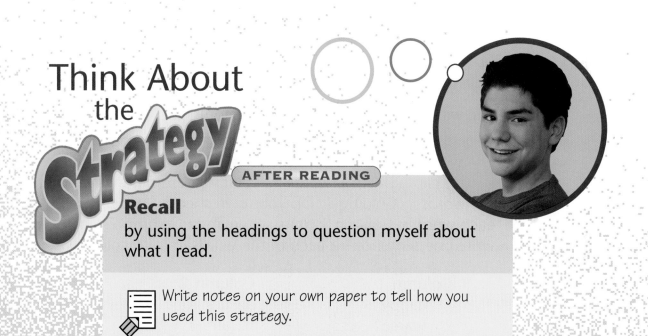

Think About the Strategy

AFTER READING

Recall

by using the headings to question myself about what I read.

Write notes on your own paper to tell how you used this strategy.

Synonyms

Synonyms are words with the same or nearly the same meaning as another word. Synonyms can make writing more interesting because the same words are not used over and over. You can find synonyms in a thesaurus. A thesaurus is like a dictionary, except instead of giving you the meaning of words, it gives synonyms and antonyms (words that have the opposite meaning).

In the selection *Jacques Cousteau: Crusader of the Sea*, you read the following sentence:

> *He was **amazed** at the things he could see!*

If you were to look up the word *amaze* in a thesaurus, you would find its synonyms. Some of the synonyms for the word *amaze* are:

> *surprise, astound, bewilder, astonish*

If you were rewriting the sentence, you could use any of the above words instead of the word *amazed*. For example:

> He was *surprised* at the things he could see!

The words in Column 1 below are different types of feelings people can have. The words in Column 2 are synonyms for the words in Column 1. On your own sheet of paper, match each word in Column 1 to its synonym in Column 2. Then, write one sentence for each of the words in both columns.

Column 1	Column 2
1. happy	a. unhappy
2. scared	b. afraid
3. sad	c. glad
4. comfortable	d. angry
5. mad	e. cozy
6. excited	f. calm
7. silly	g. thrilled
8. peaceful	h. foolish
9. friendly	i. energetic
10. lively	j. neighborly

Monologue

Do you ever wonder what life was like as Cousteau swam under the sea? Read this passage to yourself. Practice reading with fluency. Then read it aloud to a friend.

Fluency **TIP**

This monologue has many beautiful descriptions. Express your amazement at the beauty of undersea life in your voice. Pay careful attention to the punctuation.

An Underwater Dive With Cousteau

Jacques Cousteau opened our eyes to a special place—the world of the sea.

When he was underwater, what would Cousteau see? With his goggles, or an undersea mask, he could see a lot!

Cousteau often dove in shallow, warm waters near coral reefs. Many parts of the world have reefs like this. Corals are living things. They grow slowly. They build up like a town and provide food and shelter for many creatures.

Near coral reefs, Cousteau would see colorful fish. Rainbow fish and parrotfish live there. Cousteau might see squids hanging suspended in the water in groups. Sea turtles and stingrays like coral reefs, too. Without a sound, they swim past you in the water. Even the corals themselves are colorful and pretty.

Cousteau dove in deeper, colder waters, too. Many different and amazing creatures are found in the deep sea. Cousteau saw many big fish there. He saw huge octopuses and sharks.

Underwater, it is quiet. But it is not silent. Even underwater, creatures make noise. To the diver, the underwater world sounds like crackles or clicks.

Seahorses. Starfish. Jellyfish. Dolphins and whales. These are just some of the amazing creatures that Cousteau saw under the sea!

Think About the Strategies

BEFORE READING

Preview the Selection

by looking at the photographs, illustrations, captions, and graphics to predict what the selection will be about.

DURING READING

Make Connections

by comparing my experiences with what I'm reading.

AFTER READING

Recall

by using the headings to question myself about what I read.

 Use your own paper to jot notes to apply these Before, During, and After Reading Strategies. In this selection, you will choose when to stop, think, and respond.

MAE C. JEMISON: SOARING TO THE SKY

Work and fun in space

Dr. Mae Jemison is someone you should know. She made history. She was the first African American woman **astronaut**.

This is the story of how Jemison became the first African American woman to blast off into **space**!

A Goal in the Sky

Jemison grew up in Chicago, Illinois. Her parents worked hard. But money was tight. The family had to live in a poor part of town. The children could not go to the best schools.

Jemison liked to learn. The whole world interested her. She found many ways to learn. She read about nature. She learned about early life on Earth. She studied history. She watched the stars in the night sky.

Vo·cab·u·lar·y

astronaut (as•truh•nawt)— someone who explores space

space (spays)—everything outside of Earth's atmosphere, including the planets and stars

[141]

Jemison liked science and the arts. But she decided to become a scientist. The young girl had a big goal. Her goal was to go to space.

To reach a goal, you have to make plans. It might take many steps. Becoming a scientist would help Jemison reach her goal of flying to space.

Challenges

Jemison was smart. But she grew up in the 1960s. At that time, girls and African Americans were not always given much respect. Girls were not **encouraged** to study science. It was hard for African Americans to get a good education.

As Jemison was a girl *and* an African American, she faced two big **challenges**. Challenges make things extra hard to do. They are a kind of test. How could Jemison defeat these challenges? How could she prove that she would be an excellent scientist?

Working Hard

Mae Jemison faced her challenges by doing much more than others expected of her. Most people finish high school at age 18. Jemison finished 2 years earlier. She did it by plain hard work.

Stanford University heard about this smart girl. The university offered to pay for Jemison to study there. Stanford is in California. It was a big move. Jemison lived far from California. At 16 years old, she went to California, and she was on her own.

At first, it was not easy. Some teachers did not think girls did not think girls

Mae Jemison went to college at Stanford University in California.

could do the work. Some did not think African Americans could do the work. Jemison proved them all wrong. Her grades were high. She became an **engineer**.

Vo•cab•u•lar•y

encouraged (en•kur•ijd)— helped make something happen

challenges (chal•uhn•jez)— special tests or difficulties; something that requires all of a person's efforts and skills

engineer (en•juh•neer)— someone who learns how things work

Jemison did not stop there. Next, she became a doctor. Cornell University asked her to study there. It is in the state of New York. Then, she worked in West Africa for the Peace Corps, helping the sick. Again, she was far from home. But this step would get her closer to her goal. Being a doctor would help her get into space.

Astronaut-in-Training

It was the year 1987. Jemison was working as a doctor. But it was time to take the next step toward her goal. It would be her biggest step.

Jemison **applied** to NASA. NASA stands for National Aeronautics and Space Administration. NASA is the space agency of the United States. Two thousand people applied for the job of astronaut. Only Jemison and 14 other people were accepted!

Jemison moved to Houston, Texas. That is the home of NASA. She began **training** to become an astronaut.

Mae Jemison—astronaut-in-training

Astronauts are taught many things. They must know how their **spacecraft** works. They must know a lot about space. They must know a lot about Earth.

Astronauts must be strong and healthy. Going to space is hard on the body. It is hard on the mind, too. It is dangerous. Many things can go wrong. Astronauts can die. They have to be prepared for many things that might happen.

Jemison's training could be scary. As a child, she was afraid of high places. Now, NASA wanted her to jump out of planes wearing a **parachute**. Talk about high up! But Jemison fought her fear. She jumped.

To Space!

On September 12, 1992, Jemison reached her goal. She flew into space! Her hard work and training had paid off.

Vo•cab•u•lar•y

applied (uh•**plyd**)—asked for a job

training (**tray**•ning)—learning or being taught how to do things

spacecraft (**spays**•kraft)—a machine that travels beyond Earth's atmosphere

parachute (**pair**•uh•shoot)—a big piece of fabric that lets someone float gently to the ground from a great height

Jemison was onboard with six other astronauts. They flew on the *Endeavor*. It was a **space shuttle**.

To get into space, you must first leave Earth's **atmosphere**. It took *Endeavor* eight minutes to reach **orbit**. This is where a spacecraft circles Earth.

The *Endeavor* soared. As it flew through the pull of Earth's **gravity,** Jemison felt a strong force on her chest. When the shuttle reached orbit, the force lifted. She knew that the shuttle was moving very, very fast. But inside the spacecraft, it was still.

All of the astronauts felt **weightless**. They felt almost free of the pull of gravity. They were able to float. They rolled around in midair. Pencils drifted. It was great fun!

Mae Jemison, proud astronaut, poses for an official NASA portrait.

The view was fantastic. It was beautiful. The astronauts could see Earth, the sun, and the moon. Everything was clear. The stars were bright. From space, Earth looked like a big blue marble. They could see the oceans and the land.

Yes, it was fun. But everyone had lots of work to do, too.

Jemison's job was to complete science tests. She studied the effects of gravity. She looked at how weightlessness affects living things. She tested how substances like glass and metals act in space.

The astronauts spent almost 8 days in space. They traveled more than 3 million miles. They orbited Earth 126 times. It was the trip of a lifetime!

Vo•**cab**•u•lar•y

space shuttle (**spays** shut•l)—a spacecraft that travels to and from space many times

atmosphere (**at**•muh•sfeer)—the whole mass and layers of air surrounding Earth

orbit (**or**•bit)—a zone where a spacecraft circles Earth or another body in space

gravity (**grav**•i•tee)—a natural pull or force on all things in the universe

weightless (**wayt**•lis)—having little pull of gravity

No Limits

Jemison left NASA in 1993. It was time to explore other goals. She liked to find new things to learn and do.

Today, Jemison teaches young people how science can improve our lives. She especially encourages people who face special challenges, like she did. She teaches, "Don't be limited by other people's imaginations."

Jemison cares about all of us here on "Spaceship Earth." She tells us we can find ways to solve problems. And, by example, she shows that we really can reach our goals.

Highlights of Mae Jemison's Life
1956 – Mae Carol Jemison born on October 17
1973 – graduates from high school and starts college
1977 – finishes college with a degree in engineering
1981 – graduates from medical school
1983–1985 – works in West Africa for the Peace Corps
1987 – is accepted by NASA to become an astronaut
1992 – blasts into space on the *Endeavor*
1993 – leaves NASA to teach and explore other great horizons
1993–present – runs the Jemison Group, an organization created to improve science classes in schools

Blastoff!

Vocabulary

Suffixes

A **suffix** is a word part that is placed at the end of a word. A suffix changes the meaning of a word. Knowing the meaning of a suffix can give you a clue about the word's meaning.

The suffix -*less* means "without." So, for example, *windowless* means "without any windows."

In the selection *Mae C. Jemison: Soaring to the Sky,* you read the following sentence:

All of the astronauts felt **weightless.**

The word *weightless* means "without weight."

Think about how -*less* is part of the meaning of the following word:

fearless—"without fear"

The suffix -*ful* means "full of" or "having." For example, a *tasteful* recipe is "a recipe that is full of or has taste."

In *Mae C. Jemison: Soaring to the Sky,* you read the following sentence:

It was **beautiful.**

The word *beautiful* means "full of or having beauty."

Think about how -*ful* is part of the meaning of the following word:

bucketful—"the amount that fills a bucket"

Read the words in Column 1. Then add -*less* to them. Write the new words on your own piece of paper. Use each new word in a sentence. Then, read the words in Column 2 and add -*ful* to them. Write the new words and a new sentence for each word.

Column 1	Column 2
1. boot	**6.** cheer
2. hat	**7.** cap
3. care	**8.** care
4. speech	**9.** hand
5. thought	**10.** thought

Notice that the words in numbers 3 and 8, and in numbers 5 and 10 are the same. How does the suffix change the meaning of these words?

Poetry

The following poem is about Mae Jemison's trip into space. Practice this poem several times until you think you can read or say it smoothly to an audience. You might present it with a partner, taking turns with each verse.

Fluency ▶ **TIP**

The astronauts in this poem must be very excited. Be sure to show this excitement in your voice as you read the poem.

Mae Jemison's Trip

We're strapped in our seats—
We're ready to go.
The spacecraft is humming—
The fuel starts to flow.

The countdown has ended—
The spacecraft lifts off.
We're pressed in our seats from
The force of the loft.

Once we reach orbit
The pressure lets up.
We float in the shuttle,
Then break for our sup.

Outside of our windows
The moon wanders past.
Earth starts to shrink—
We're moving so fast!

It's now time for work—
We ready our tests.
We hope to improve life
For all of the rest.

Our mission complete,
We streak back to Earth.
Our space journey's over—
We've proven our worth!

List

Conservation: Helping the Environment

The environment is our natural world. It includes all living things, the water, the air, and the soil. We should all help conserve Earth's resources. To conserve means "to take care of all natural things." We must protect them and keep them safe from harm.

What can we do to conserve the environment?
We can—

1. Plant new trees to replace trees we use to make homes and buildings. This keeps the forests healthy.

2. Turn off lights when we leave a room. This saves energy.

3. Recycle cans, glass, and newspapers. This saves natural resources such as trees.

4. Waste less water. The water we do not use helps animals, trees, and plants.

5. Take care of and protect the habitats of wildlife. We do not want to lose any more species.

6. Buy nonaerosol products. This protects the ozone layer.

7. Buy and use products that are not tested on animals. This protects the lives and health of our animals and wildlife.

8. Make a compost pile of peels from fruits and vegetables. This keeps the land healthy.

9. Walk, ride bikes, or ride the bus whenever possible. We do not use so much gasoline that way. Gasoline makes the air dirty.

10. Throw away our trash properly. We do not want to litter the environment.

We can all be good citizens and make the world a better place.

Discussion Questions

Answer these questions with a partner or on a separate sheet of paper.

1. Why must we plant new trees?

2. What makes the environment?

3. Why must you never put trash into the ocean?

4. Which of the following things cannot be recycled?
   a. cans
   b. aerosol products
   c. newspapers
   d. glass

5. After eating dinner, which of the ten steps toward conservation can you do?
   a. Buy nonaerosol products.
   b. Take care of the habitats of wildlife.
   c. Make a compost pile from the peels of the fruits and vegetables you ate.
   d. Plant new trees.

6. Which of the following is a natural resource?
   a. trees
   b. homes
   c. bikes
   d. lights

7. Where do wild animals live?
   a. rooms
   b. habitats
   c. buildings
   d. ozone layer

8. What is a compost pile?

CONNECTING
to the Real World

EXPLORE MORE

Start a Nature Journal

Every day you can write about something you explored in nature. Maybe you took a walk in the rain. Maybe you saw an interesting bug. Use your senses of touch, sight, sound, and smell to write about your experiences.

Plan an Event

Organize a cleanup day at a local park. Ask your friends and classmates to help. This project can help keep the environment clean.

Create a Map

Get a map of the United States. Mark the location of each of the big national parks: Yosemite, Crater Lake, Everglades, Glacier, Mount Rushmore, etc. Use colorful markers.

Make a Chart

Make a chart with the name of each of your family members. Use a different color for each person. Count the minutes each person spends in the shower each day. Write the numbers on the chart. Encourage your family to reduce the time. Everyone must be careful about conserving water.

Make a Fish Mobile

Make your fish by cutting out paper triangles. Cut out one big triangle for the fish's body. Cut two smaller triangles for fins. Cut a circle for an eye and a circle for the mouth. Glue the parts together. Make several paper fish. Then color them in using many colors. Cut out small circles at the top of each fish and attach strings through them. Hang your fish mobile in your room at home or in your classroom. It will remind you of some of the living things found in the ocean.

Decorate Your Library

You and your classmates can draw colorful pictures to decorate the local library. The drawings can be about the planets and stars. This can help people remember the mysteries of space.

Related Books

Barr, Linda. *Jacques Cousteau: Ocean Explorer.* Zaner-Bloser, 2004.

Black, Sonia W. *Mae Jemison.* Mondo Publishing, 2000.

Burby, Liza N. *Mae Jemison: The First African American Woman Astronaut.* Powerkids Press, 1998.

Drake, Jane, and Ann Love. *Forestry.* Kids Can Press, 1998.

Fife, Dale H. *The Empty Lot.* Little, Brown and Company, 1991.

Hopping, Lorraine Jean. *Jacques Cousteau: Saving Our Seas.* McGraw-Hill/ Contemporary Books, 2000.

Jemison, Mae. *Find Where the Wind Goes.* Scholastic, 2001.

King, Roger. *Jacques Cousteau and the Undersea World (Explorers of New Worlds).* Chelsea House Publishing, 2000.

Kowalski, Kathiann M. *The Everything Kids' Nature Book.* Adams Media Corporation, 2000.

Maze, Stephanie, and Catherine O'Neill. *I Want to Be . . . An Environmentalist.* Harcourt, Inc. 2000.

Muir, John. *John Muir: My Life With Nature (Sharing Nature With Children Book).* Dawn Publications, 2000.

Naden, Corrine, and Rose Blue. *John Muir, Saving the Wilderness.* The Millbrook Press, 1992.

Putnam, Jeff. *Explorers of the Earth.* Zaner-Bloser, 2004.

—*Explorers of the Oceans.* Zaner-Bloser, 2004.

—*Explorers of the Sky.* Zaner-Bloser, 2004.

Ring, Elizabeth. *Rachel Carson: Caring for the Earth.* The Millbrook Press, 1994.

Steele, Christy. *Oceans.* Steck-Vaughn Company, 2001.

Wishinsky, Frieda. *The Man Who Made Parks: The Story of Parkbuilder Frederick Law Olmsted.* Tundra Books, 1999.

Interesting Web Sites

John Muir and Explorations on Land
www.sierraclub.org/john_muir_exhibit/frameindex.html?
http://www.sierraclub.org/john_muir_exhibit/bibliographic_resources/john_muir_
 bibliography/childrens_books.html

Jacques Cousteau and Explorations of the Sea
www.cousteausociety.org/tsc_people.html
www.divediscover.whoi.edu/
www.enchantedlearning.com/themes/dolphins.shtml
www.enchantedlearning.com/explorers/undersea.shtml

Mae Jemison and Explorations of the Sky
www.ci.hickory.nc.us/library/Photo_sessions/jemison/drmaejemison.htm
www.enchantedlearning.com/explorers/page/j/jemison.shtml

Web sites have been carefully researched for accuracy, content, and appropriateness. However, teachers and caregivers are reminded that Web sites are subject to change. Internet use should always be monitored.

BEFORE READING

Activate Prior Knowledge

by reading the introduction and/or summary to decide what I know about this topic.

DURING READING

Interact With Text

by identifying how the text is organized.

AFTER READING

Evaluate

by forming a judgment about whether the selection was objective or biased.

LEARN
the **strategies**
in the selection
Hurricanes
page 155

PRACTICE
the **strategies**
in the selection
Lightning
page 167

APPLY
the **strategies**
in the selection
Sandstorms
page 177

Think About
the
Strategies

BEFORE READING

Activate Prior Knowledge

by reading the introduction and/or summary to decide what I know about this topic.

My Thinking

The strategy says to read the introduction and/or summary to decide what I know about this topic. The introduction in italics gives some words for a hurricane and describes what happens during this kind of storm. I've seen storms like that on television, and I know that they're scary. Now I'll read on to see if I'm right and to see what more they tell me about these storms.

DURING READING

Interact With Text

by identifying how the text is organized.

My Thinking

The strategy says to identify how the text is organized. I will stop and think about this strategy every time I come to a red button like this ●.

Hurricanes

A satellite photo of a hurricane
and its eye

A monster! A terrible killer storm! Winds zoom faster than 74 miles per hour. Heavy rains may fall. One storm can crush thousands of homes. The damage can cost billions of dollars.

What is a hurricane? It is a kind of **cyclone** that starts out at sea. Cyclones are strong windstorms. In the Atlantic Ocean, they are called hurricanes. They are called **typhoons** in the Pacific and Indian Oceans.

The word *hurricane* came from the West Indies. The West Indies is a group of islands between Florida and the northern coast of South America. Long ago, Carib Indians there called this storm a *hurican*. That was the name of their evil god.

Since 1953, each hurricane has gotten a name. In the beginning, they were all given girls' names. Now, boys' names are used, too.

Vo·cab·u·lar·y

cyclone (sy•klohn)—a strong storm that brings heavy winds and rain

typhoons (ty•foonz)—tropical cyclones in the western Pacific Ocean or Indian Ocean

[155]

Strategy

Interact With Text
by identifying how the text is organized.

My Thinking
The text in this article is organized with questions and answers. I notice that the question "How Do Hurricanes Form?" is asked in the heading. Then the answer about water temperature rising and the winds blowing a certain way is given.

Vo·cab·u·lar·y

tropical (**trop**•i•kuhl)—located in a hot, wet part of the world called the tropics

islands (**eye**•luhndz)—bodies of land that are surrounded by water

temperature (**tem**•puhr•uh•chur)—degree of hotness or coldness

counterclockwise (**kown**•tuhr•**klok**•wyz)—moving from right to left instead of clockwise (left to right) like the hands of a clock

eye—the quietest part of the storm

moisture (**moys**•chuhr)—liquid, such as water, that is in the air or on the ground; wetness

How Do Hurricanes Form?

Hurricanes are **tropical** storms. Many start near the coast of Africa. These storms move across the Atlantic Ocean. Some become hurricanes. They may hit **islands**. Others strike in the Gulf of Mexico. The Gulf of Mexico is part of the Atlantic Ocean that borders the southeast coast of the United States. It stretches from Texas in the west to Florida in the east. Mexico is on its southern border. Some hurricanes hit the coast of North or Central America.

Most North Atlantic hurricanes strike in summer and early fall. The hurricane season runs from June through November.

Hurricanes need warm ocean water. The water **temperature** must be at least 80°F. The winds must blow a certain way. The winds gather over the warm sea, building up speed. The winds spin **counterclockwise**. They move around a center. That center is called the **eye**. It is the calmest part of the storm. Most eyes are 15 to 20 miles around in size.

Bands of clouds form around the eye. These clouds are cooler than the eye. They hold **moisture**. Rain fills the clouds. The rain lets out some heat. This heat loss keeps the winds strong.

The fast-moving air helps build up clouds. Some storms grow huge. A cloud mass can stretch for 2,000 miles.

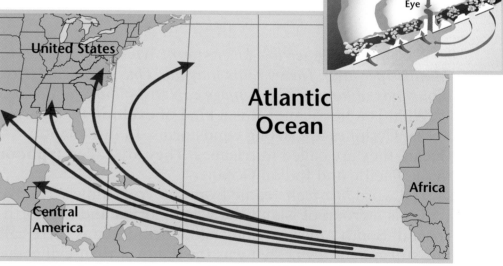

ABOVE: Many hurricanes form near the coast of Africa and move across the Atlantic Ocean.
INSET: Winds spin counterclockwise around the eye of a hurricane.

Who Looks Out for Storms?

Long ago, people did not know when a big storm was coming. That began to change in the 1950s. Scientists began to use special tools to study the weather. Now, they can **predict** storms better.

The National Hurricane Center (NHC) is based in Florida. People at the NHC track storms. They try to spot them early. The NHC tells people when hurricanes are coming.

Storm Coming!

Radio and TV reports spread the news. People may be told to leave the area. They pack things they will need during the storm. Some head for a shelter. Others stay at hotels or with friends. Cars and buses jam the roads. Airports are crowded, too.

In 1992, Hurricane Andrew hit Florida. More than 500,000 people left before the storm. But some stayed to watch their homes. They hoped they could stay safe there.

Strategy

Interact With Text by identifying how the text is organized.

My Thinking
I notice that the question "Who Looks Out for Storms?" is asked in the heading. Then the answer "National Hurricane Center" is given. Again, the text in this article is organized as questions and answers.

People at the National Hurricane Center work hard to track storms.

Vo•cab•u•lar•y

predict (pri•**dikt**)—
to know or guess what might happen

Strategy

Interact With Text
by identifying how the text is organized.

My Thinking
I notice that the question "What Happens During the Storm?" is asked in the heading. Then the answer about winds causing damage and water causing flooding is given. It also tells where they can hit and how they can move.

What Happens During the Storm?

Hurricanes are scary. Winds scream like loud trains. Walls shake. People fear their homes will blow away. Some do. The doors fly off. Glass shatters. The roof falls apart and rain gushes inside.

On the streets, cars bounce around. Trees and power lines collapse. Even airplanes are smashed.

Water can flood the coast or **inland** areas. Some storms bring more than six inches of rain. Winds can drag ocean water onto land. Streets look like rivers.

A hurricane can hit more than one place. Some move from state to state. Big storms may last for days or weeks. They can leave a terrible trail of destruction.

After the Storm

Much work starts when a hurricane ends. Some victims are trapped under the **rubble**. Search dogs help workers find them. Other people need medical care. They have broken bones and cuts.

People need food, clean water, and clothing. Keeping clean is another problem. Some people are homeless. Phones do not work and power lines are down. Roads are closed. People cannot get to work and children cannot go to school.

Victims are scared and sad. They face many losses. Their homes lie in ruins. They look around. Maybe there is something left? A toy or photo seems very precious.

Other people come to help. Many are Red Cross workers. The Red Cross is a charity group that helps victims of hurricanes, floods, wars, and other disasters. They set up shelters. They bring fresh water and food. The Red Cross has collected money from all around the world. It is used to help victims. Members of other charity organizations, such as the American Society for the Prevention of Cruelty to Animals (ASPCA) help, too. They reunite pets with their owners. They also care for animals until owners can be found.

Cleaning up after a storm can take a long time. It costs a lot of money.

Workers help bring supplies to victims.

Vo·cab·u·lar·y

inland (in•luhnd)—located in the interior, or away from the coast

rubble (rub•uhl)—broken or crumbled material that is left when a building falls down

How Are Storms Ranked?

New hurricanes form each year. They are ranked and given a class number from 1 to 5. Faster winds mean a higher class number. Class 1 is a weak storm. It may harm some plants and trees. Class 2 is more serious. Class 3 is even worse. It destroys trailers and damages homes. Tall trees fall over. A Class 4 storm damages land, trees, and buildings. Class 5 storms are the worst.

Heavy rains destroyed these crops in Florida.

Strategy

Interact With Text by identifying how the text is organized.

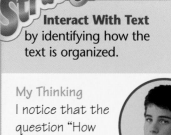

My Thinking
I notice that the question "How Are Storms Ranked?" is asked in the heading. Then the answer, "They are given a class number from 1 to 5," is given.

Hurricane Agnes, a Class 1 storm, struck in June 1972. It hit the Atlantic Coast. Twenty-two people died. Pennsylvania was hit the hardest.

In 1992, Andrew hit South Florida. It was even worse than Agnes. Andrew was a Class 4 storm. Wind speeds reached 140 miles per hour.

Camille was a Class 5 storm. It slammed into the Gulf Coast in 1969. Wind speeds hit 200 miles per hour. That was the worst storm ever to hit North America.

Hurricane Camille left many people homeless.

Strategy

Interact With Text
by identifying how the text is organized.

My Thinking

The question "Can People Stay Safe?" is asked in the heading. Then the answer, about scientists being better able to see storms coming, is given. Again, the text is organized into questions and answers.

Can People Stay Safe?

Hurricanes cause big problems. Yet fewer people die from them these days. In 1900, a Texas hurricane caused 6,000 deaths. Fewer than 50 people died during Hurricane Andrew.

Nobody can stop these storms. But now people know more about them and have more time to get away. Technology plays a big roll in reducing the number of deaths from hurricanes. Today, radar and satellites track storms. Scientists are better able to see a storm coming. Today's better and faster means of communication help inform people about how to protect themselves.

Helping Others

What can you do to help others after a hurricane? Contact the Red Cross to find out what they need. Perhaps adults in your family can donate blood to that organization. You may be asked to send blankets, nonperishable foods, or other supplies. Perhaps they'll want other kinds of donations.

Check with your teacher, too. Your class may be able to send cards or letters to families or schools. Your support can be valuable in many ways.

Red Cross workers give food and water to hurricane victims.

How Can You Stay Safe?

A national weather organization, known as the National Weather Service, says that the best thing you can do is be "informed and prepared" for a storm. You can do five things to help prevent a disaster:

- Develop a family plan
- Create a Disaster Supply Kit
- Have a place to go
- Make your home safe
- Make your pet safe

For information about the National Hurricane Center's suggestions, your parents can go to www.nhc.noaa.gov.

Hurricanes are a strong force of nature that can cause death and destruction. But, the more people know, the better they can prepare. And, the more they prepare, the safer they will be.

Think About the Strategy

AFTER READING

Evaluate
by forming a judgment about whether the selection was objective or biased.

My Thinking

The strategy says to evaluate by forming a judgment about whether the selection was objective or biased. This means I must decide if the article was fair and written from facts. The selection refers to suggestions from the National Weather Service and the National Hurricane Center, which are official weather services. I believe that makes this an objective selection.

Also, I can check the facts in this selection with other articles in newspapers and magazines. That makes me sure this selection is objective and not biased.

Graphic organizers help us organize information. I chose an outline as my graphic organizer for "Hurricanes." An outline uses roman numerals, capital letters, and numerals to organize the information. The roman numerals show how I'm going to organize my summary. The capital letters show supporting ideas, and the numerals below the capital letters show the details. I will be able to write my introduction, body, and summary from this outline.

Outline
Hurricanes

I. **Introduction**

    A. A hurricane is a kind of cyclone that starts out at sea.

    B. These strong storms are called hurricanes in the Atlantic Ocean.

    C. They are called typhoons in the Pacific and Indian Oceans.

II. **Body**

    A. How do hurricanes form?

        1. They start near warm ocean water.

        2. The winds blow a certain way and build up speed.

        3. They spin counterclockwise.

        4. They move around a center.

        5. Bands of clouds form around the eye.

        6. Rain fills the clouds.

    B. Who looks out for storms?

        1. The National Hurricane Center (NHC) predicts hurricanes.

        2. Radio and TV reporters spread the news.

    C. How can people help?

        1. Organizations such as the Red Cross collect money, set up shelters, and provide fresh food and water.

        2. The ASPCA takes care of pets.

        3. People can donate blood and send blankets and food.

III. **Summary**

    A. Hurricanes are dangerous.

    B. People will be better prepared if they know more about hurricanes.

    C. People will be safer if they are better prepared.

I used my graphic organizer to write a summary of the article. Can you find the information in my summary that came from my outline?

A Summary of
Hurricanes

A hurricane is a kind of cyclone that starts out at sea. These strong storms are called hurricanes in the Atlantic Ocean. They are called typhoons in the Pacific and Indian Oceans.

How do hurricanes form? They start near warm ocean water, at least 80 degrees F. Then as the winds blow, they build up speed. They spin counterclockwise. They move around a center, called an eye. Bands of clouds form around the eye. Rain fills the clouds.

Who looks out for storms? Hurricanes can be predicted by the National Hurricane Center (NHC). They use special tools to see hurricanes coming. Also, reporters look out for storms. They want to make sure that people know the storm is coming. People in the storm's path will need to seek shelter.

How can people help? Organizations such as the Red Cross help by collecting money, setting up shelters, and providing fresh food and water. The ASPCA rescues pets. They help take care of the pets until they are reunited with their owners. People can donate blood and send blankets and nonperishable food.

Hurricanes are dangerous storms. They can be very scary. But there are things people can do to be ready. If we know more about how and where hurricanes form, we can be ready and prepared. We will be safe if we are prepared and ready.

Introduction
My introductory paragraph tells readers what they are about to read.

Body
I used information from my outline to write my body paragraphs. My first body paragraph tells how hurricanes form. My second body paragraph tells who looks out for the storms. My third body paragraph tells how people can help.

Conclusion
I summarized my paper by recalling some of the main ideas.

Similes

A **simile** is used by a writer to compare two unlike things. A simile is a kind of figurative language. It helps you picture what the writer is describing. A simile uses the words *like* or *as* to compare.

In "Hurricanes," you read the following sentence:
> ***Streets*** *look* ***like*** ***rivers***.

The author compared the water on the street during a hurricane to water flowing in a river. The author used the word *like* to make the comparison.

Read these other similes. Notice that each one compares a person to something in nature.

1. The young man is *like* a vulture at the dinner table.

2. Jackson is *like* a huge, frozen mountain.

3. During the chess game, Walker was as cold *as* a stone to his opponent.

On your own sheet of paper, write the following sentences. Then, write down the two unlike things that are being compared. For example, for the three sentences above you would write,

young man = vulture
Jackson = huge, frozen mountain
Walker = stone

1. In the courtroom, she can strike as quickly as a shark.

2. His smile was as bright as the sun.

3. At the track meet, Michelle ran as quickly as a gazelle.

4. Peter is like a rock to his ill father.

5. On the stage, she is as graceful as a swan.

Readers' Theater

In a small group, practice reading this dialogue. When you're ready, read it aloud to the class.

Fluency ►**TIP**

Read this passage silently and then talk with your classmates about how Ben, Mr. Jackson, and the TV announcer are feeling. When you read, express your character's feelings through your voice.

Eye of the Storm

Narrator: A warning is sounding on the television. Beep . . . beep.

Ben: Dad, look! There's news about the hurricane!

TV Announcer: The hurricane is getting closer. It is now moving up from the West Indies into the Gulf of Mexico. Right now it's ranked a Class 3 hurricane, but it could turn into a 4. This storm could be very bad, especially on the islands off the coast.

Ben: Dad, I'm worried. I've read about hurricanes in school. A number 4 isn't very good. What should we do now?

Mr. Jackson: Don't worry. We've already boarded up the windows and taken other precautions, so the house should be fine. We'll drive inland to your aunt's house. We'll wait out the storm there.

TV Announcer: This storm is passing over waters with high temperatures. It's going to bring a lot of moisture to the area. There is a chance of severe flooding. You might want to go to a shelter.

Narrator: Ben and his father pack some clothes. They put their pet bunny in a carrier and start shutting up the house.

Ben: Dad, do you have our emergency kit?

Mr. Jackson: Yes, Ben. It's in the car and ready to go. We also have bottled water and some food.

Ben: OK, Dad. I have Bunny and some food for her. We're ready to go.

TV Announcer: The National Hurricane Center predicts that the eye of the hurricane will pass right over our area.

Mr. Jackson: Let's turn off the news. We've done all we can to prepare. We'll be safe at your aunt's house. Now it's all up to nature.

Narrator: Ben and his father paid attention to the warnings from the National Hurricane Center. When they came back a few days later, they saw that their home had withstood the hurricane!

Think About

the

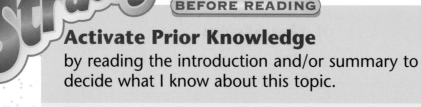

Strategies

BEFORE READING

Activate Prior Knowledge

by reading the introduction and/or summary to decide what I know about this topic.

Write notes on your own paper to tell how you used this strategy.

DURING READING

Interact With Text

by identifying how the text is organized.

 When you come to a red button like this ◉, write notes on your own paper to tell how you used this strategy.

Lightning

A bolt of lightning splits the sky.

Flash! An intense line of white splits the sky. The whole world lights up. It's *lightning!*

When a **bolt** of lightning appears, the world gets brighter. Even from inside your house, you can often see that something big has happened. Light flashes on the walls. Nature is putting on a show. It does not matter how often you see it. Lightning always gets your attention. It is one of the most wonderful sights in nature. But it is also dangerous.

Vo•**cab**•u•lar•y

bolt (bohlt)—a stroke or line of lightning

Strategy

Interact With Text by identifying how the text is organized.

Write notes on your own paper to tell how you used this strategy.

Inventor Benjamin Franklin studied lightning. In 1752, he used a kite to do tests during a storm.

What Causes Lightning?

Lightning is a kind of **electrical charge**. It starts in the clouds, when different layers of ice **crystals** run into each other.

There are many kinds of lightning. Lightning might be just a single jagged line. Or it might look like a tree with many branches. Lightning never looks the exact same way twice. The lightning may stay completely within one cloud. It might stretch from one cloud to another. Or it might travel from a cloud down toward the ground.

Vo·**cab**·u·lar·y

electrical charge (i•**lek**•tri•kuhl **chahrj**)— a natural burst of power or energy

crystals (**kris**•tuhlz)—tiny, transparent pieces

[**168**]

Sometimes lightning looks like the branches of a tree.

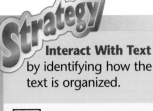
Interact With Text by identifying how the text is organized.

Write notes on your own paper to tell how you used this strategy.

Each lightning flash lasts less than a second. It is so bright, though, that we might think it lasts longer.

Sometimes you will see lightning again and again in a short time. That means a big storm is nearby. At other times, you see just a few bolts of lightning. That means the storm is ending, or, it is too far away for you to see all the lightning.

Dry lightning sometimes starts forest fires.

What Is Dry Lightning?

Lightning usually happens in rain clouds. But there is also something called dry lightning. It starts in clouds that do not carry rain.

Dry lightning is dangerous. It can cause fires. That's because there is no rain to put out a fire. Dry lightning is most **hazardous** if it **strikes** a tree in the forest. It can start a large forest fire.

Vo•cab•u•lar•y

hazardous (haz•uhr•duhs)— full of danger

strikes (stryks)—hits

[169]

What Is That Sound?

Suddenly, a loud sound fills the air. Crack! Boom! Rumble.

Doors and windows rattle. The cat crouches low and runs to hide under the bed. The dog rushes to your side for **protection**. Everyone notices. They stop what they are doing.

Big sounds can happen with lightning. These sounds are called **thunder**. Lightning is very hot, and the heating of the air along its path causes thunder.

If the thunder is really loud (a big crack! or a boom!), it means the storm is close to you. The lightning might be right above your neighborhood! If the thunder seems quieter, the lightning is probably farther away.

Thunder can tell you how close lightning is. When you see a bolt of lightning, start counting. For every five seconds that you count before you hear thunder, the lightning is one mile away. So, if ten seconds pass before you hear thunder, the lightning is two miles away. If thunder and lightning happen at almost the same time, it means the lightning is very close.

Vo·**cab**·u·lar·y

protection (pruh•**tek**•shuhn) —being kept safe from harm

thunder (**thun**•duhr)—noise from shock waves created by the heat along the path of lightning

The sound of thunder can tell you if lightning is nearby.

Will You See Lightning Today?

Most people do not see lightning every day. But somewhere on Earth, there is always lightning. Around the world, lightning strikes 100 times each second! Lightning strikes someplace on Earth more than 8 million times per day!

Lightning is most common in warm weather. But it can appear even during snowstorms.

How Can You Protect Yourself?

About 1,000 people around the world are killed by lightning each year. Many more are badly hurt. Being struck by lightning can hurt your heart and your head. Some people lose their memories. Some may feel the effects of a lightning strike for a long time.

But you can do things to protect yourself from lightning. You can be prepared.

The first thing to do is to pay attention to weather **reports**. Every day newspapers report about the weather. There are always weather reports on the radio and television, too. It is smart to listen to them. They tell you if a storm with lightning is coming. You will know when it is time to go inside.

If a storm with lightning comes near, you want to be indoors. Go inside a building. You can sit in a car, too. Just be sure to keep the windows up. Try not to touch things that are made of metal. If you are swimming, get out of the water.

Inside, you still have to take some steps to be safe. Many things can **attract** lightning. Stay away from things like water faucets and pipes. Don't sit next to windows, in case the lightning comes close. Turn off the television. Shut down the computer. Unplug them, if you can. Don't talk on the telephone.

Strategy

Interact With Text by identifying how the text is organized.

Write notes on your own paper to tell how you used this strategy.

Lightning Do's and Don'ts

Do	Don't
Pay attention to reports	Touch things made of metal
Go inside	Swim
Keep windows closed	Use water faucets
Unplug TVs and computers	Sit next to windows
	Talk on the telephone

Vo•cab•u•lar•y

reports (ri•**ports**)—information; news stories

attract (uh•**trakt**)—to draw or pull something toward you

Interact With Text
by identifying how the
text is organized.

Write notes on your
own paper to tell how
you used this strategy.

What Is the Lightning Crouch?

What if you are outdoors and no buildings or cars are around? You can still prepare. Take off your watch, rings, and other metal things. Stay away from trees, water towers, and other tall things. All of these things attract lightning. Find a ditch or another low point in the ground. You want to be as low and as small as possible. This will keep you from attracting lightning.

Do the lightning crouch. Make yourself as small as you can. Cover your ears with your arms and crouch down. Stay on the balls of your feet.

It takes a little practice to do the lightning crouch. You might fall over at first. Practice with your family and friends. Each time you do it, you will get stronger!

The lightning crouch

The Beauty of Lightning

Yes, lightning is dangerous. And yes, we must be prepared so that it does not hurt us.

But lightning is a beautiful part of the natural world. It is wonderful to see the flashes of lightning and to hear the booms and rumbles of thunder. They remind us of the power of nature. From a safe distance, we can enjoy this exciting show.

Think About the Strategy

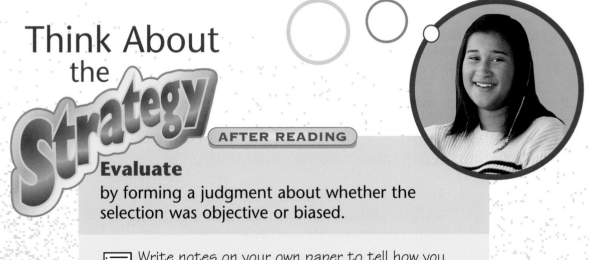

AFTER READING

Evaluate

by forming a judgment about whether the selection was objective or biased.

 Write notes on your own paper to tell how you used this strategy.

Adjectives That Compare

An **adjective** is a word that describes. Some adjectives compare two things, ideas, or people. Adjectives that compare two things are created by adding *–er* to the base word. For example, add *–er* to round to make *rounder*. Other examples include *brighter* (from bright) and *cleaner* (from clean).

In "Lightning," you read the following passage:

> *If the thunder seems quieter, the lightning is*
> *probably farther away.*

The word *quieter* was formed by adding *–er* to *quiet*. In this sentence, the sound of the thunder now is being compared to the sound of the thunder earlier.

Read the following sentences. In each, a comparison is made about the weather. The adjective that compares and what is being compared is shown after each sentence.

1. Thunder is louder than lightning.
   louder—thunder is compared to lightning
2. Rain falls faster than snow.
   faster—rain is compared to snow
3. The sun shines longer in the summer than in the winter.
   longer—sunshine in the summer is compared to sunshine in the winter

---

A comparison is being made in each of the following sentences. On your own piece of paper, write the word that is the adjective that compares. Then, write a brief description of what is being compared (as in the examples above).

1. Snow falls softer than sleet.
2. The wind blows harder in the country than in the city.
3. Clouds are darker before a storm than after a storm.
4. Rain showers are shorter in the Southwest than in the Northeast.
5. The temperature rises higher at the equator than at the poles.

Interview

Have you ever thought about what it might be like to talk to Benjamin Franklin? With a classmate, practice reading this make-believe interview. Rehearse using good fluency and expression. When you're ready, read it aloud to the class.

Fluency TIP

After you have practiced this script with a partner, record your performance on a tape recorder. Then, listen to the tape. Discuss how well you did and what you need to do to improve.

Interviewer: Dr. Franklin, you are a well-known writer, philosopher, and statesman. Why are you so interested in lightning?

Dr. Benjamin Franklin: I'm curious about the natural world. I wanted to know more about lightning. As you know, lightning is common. But it is also dangerous. It is a very powerful force of nature.

Interviewer: I hear that you have conducted many experiments. What did you learn in your experiments?

Dr. Franklin: I learned that lightning is a form of electricity. It is a strong electrical charge. Also, there are different types of lightning. It never looks the same way twice. There is even dry lightning.

Interviewer: Everyone is talking about your experiments with kites. What did you do in your kite experiments?

Dr. Franklin: I attached a piece of metal to a kite. I flew the kite during a big thunderstorm. I thought the metal would attract lightning. I was right. The metal did attract a big bolt of lightning! I'm lucky to be alive!

Interviewer: You are known for inventing the lightning rod. What is that?

Dr. Franklin: A lightning rod attracts lightning away from things that can be hurt or destroyed—like people, animals, trees, and buildings. It is a tall metal thing that you plant in the ground to attract lightning. The lightning rod makes things "grounded."

Interviewer: What a great idea! How did you think of this, Dr. Franklin?

Dr. Franklin: I just looked around me and thought about what I saw. I applied my knowledge and conducted experiments. The world is ours to explore!

Think About
the
Strategies

BEFORE READING

Activate Prior Knowledge

by reading the introduction and/or summary to decide what I know about this topic.

DURING READING

Interact With Text

by identifying how the text is organized.

AFTER READING

Evaluate

by forming a judgment about whether the selection was objective or biased.

 Use your own paper to jot notes to apply these Before, During, and After Reading Strategies. In this selection, you will choose when to stop, think, and respond.

Sandstorms

Powerful sandstorms blow across the land.

A strong wind blows the sand on the ground. The sand rises in the air. The blowing sand stings. A sandstorm is coming.

The flags at the baseball game flapped. Carlos Martinez felt the wind blow against his face. The strong winds made him close his eyes. The wind blew puffs of sand along the ground.

Mrs. Martinez yelled to Carlos. She wanted to go home right away. A sandstorm was coming. The wind roared. Carlos could not hear her yell. She grabbed his hand. Together, they ran across the field to their farmhouse.

What Is a Sandstorm?

A sandstorm is a kind of storm. A storm is a **violent** change in the air around us. A storm brings strong winds. The blowing sand is thick in the air. It is hard to see.

Clouds of sand block the sun. The sky and the ground become the same color.

How Powerful Are Sandstorms?

In a sandstorm, it is hard to get around. Strong winds blow sand into cars. People cannot drive. Sand gets into the engines of airplanes so they cannot fly. Sometimes sand covers roads and buries them.

The sand gets so thick in the air that people lose **visibility**. They cannot see the way in front of them. They can get lost. The wind can knock them down. The swirling sand stings their faces.

The force of a storm is strong. The speed of the winds is fast. Winds can **gust** up to 60 miles per hour. Cars on the highway go that fast.

The winds make the sand fly into the air. The sand grains jump and bounce around. This is called **saltation**. The blowing sand travels in columns. The sand whirls around and around. These columns can be 10 feet high or even higher. The columns can rise as high as a house.

Over time sandstorms change Earth. They change the way Earth looks. Over thousands of years, sandstorms form rocks into different shapes. In the desert, sandstorms make interesting patterns in the sand. The force of a sandstorm can move a sand dune.

What Makes the Wind Blow?

Wind is a large amount of moving air. What causes it to move?

One big cause is the sun. The sun heats Earth. But Earth is not all the same temperature. The different temperatures of the air and Earth make the air move.

Air moves at different speeds. Strong winds can start when a lot of cold air moves fast across dry ground.

The powerful winds of a sandstorm scatter sand around the world. Sand that was once in Africa can end up in Europe. It can even land in the bottom of the ocean.

Sandstorms shape rocks and sand dunes.

Vo•cab•u•lar•y

violent (**vy**•uh•luhnt)—with a lot of power and strength

visibility (viz•uh•**bil**•i•tee)— being able to see

gust —to blow in a strong sudden burst

saltation (sal•**tay**•shuhn)— the act of leaping, jumping, or dancing

Earth is not the only planet with sandstorms. Scientists study the stars. They watch what is happening on other planets in space. Mars is a planet that has sandstorms. Like Earth, scientists say, these storms occur only at certain times of the year.

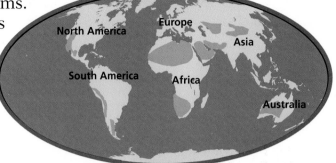

Which continents have sandstorms?

The Haboob Wind

Scientists name winds. Naming helps describe the wind. It helps show the kind of sandstorm the wind might make.

The *haboob* is the name of one wind. It means "violent wind" in Arabic. It is hot and **moist**. In the Sahara Desert, a haboob can blow huge amounts of sand.

The sand moves in a thick wall. It looks like a wave. Sometimes the wall of sand stands six miles high. A haboob can also bring thunderstorms.

Where Are the Sandstorms?

Usually, sandstorms occur in dry places. Most sandstorms occur in the **desert**. A desert is a dry area of land. It is covered with sand. In the United States, sandstorms can occur in the Mojave Desert in California. They also occur along the dry **flatlands** of Texas.

Other countries have many more sandstorms. China, Afghanistan, the Sudan, and Australia are countries that have many sandstorms.

When Do Sandstorms Happen?

Sandstorms occur at different times of the year. Summer sandstorms occur in Saudi Arabia and the United States.

A few winters ago, a mixture of sand and ice made a bad sandstorm in India and Russia. Iraq has many sandstorms in the spring. A sandy cloud covers the cities there.

Not all sandstorms are the same. Not all winds are the same. Some are hot and **humid**. Others are dry and cool.

How Do We Spot Sandstorms?

Did you ever wonder why it rains? Why does a bright blue sky suddenly change color before a storm?

Vo•cab•u•lar•y

moist (moyst)—a little wet

desert (dez•uhrt)—a large area of dry land covered with sand

flatlands (flat•landz)—flat, dry land

humid (hyoo•mid)—when the air is full of moisture and it feels like it's about to rain

Meteorologists use radar to learn about a sandstorm.

If you asked yourself these questions, you are thinking like a **meteorologist**. Meteorologists like to learn about Earth's weather. They help predict the weather.

Knowing the weather helps people plan. When the weather is going to change, meteorologists warn us. Learning about the patterns of weather keeps us safe.

Radar is one tool that meteorologists use to study weather. Weather stations, called **satellites,** are launched into space. They fly around Earth with radar cameras. The cameras take pictures of storms.

The pictures are sent to Earth. They tell when and where a storm begins. They show how fast the storm moves. They also show where it is going.

Protection in a Sandstorm

A camel is a good animal to travel with in a storm. Outside the United States, people who live in the desert have used camels for thousands of years. The camel's body helps it **adapt** to the desert. Camels have long, thick eyelashes. People have one row of lashes around each eye. Camels have two rows. The camel's eyelashes help protect its eyes from blowing sand. Sand cannot blow into the camel's eyes.

People who live in the desert also need to cover up. They wear long scarves and clothes wrapped around their head, face, and neck. Only a small opening shows their eyes. Another small opening for their nose lets them breathe.

Vo•cab•u•lar•y

meteorologist (mee•tee•uh•**rol**•uh•jist)— scientist who studies the weather

radar (**ray**•dahr)—uses radio waves to tell about faraway objects

satellites (**sat**•l•yts)—travel around Earth in space

adapt (**uh**•dapt)—to change for a reason

How do people and camels keep safe when sand blows?

Sandstorms Then and Now

When did sandstorms start on Earth? Scientists look for clues. Clues tell us about sandstorms a long time ago. They believe sandstorms happened when dinosaurs roamed Earth.

Many dinosaur **fossils** have been found in the Gobi Desert in China. Many sandstorms occur there, too. Some scientists think the sandstorms killed many dinosaurs. Then the blowing sand covered them up. The sandstorm buried the dinosaur bones. Sand **preserved** the bones.

People have always worried about sandstorms. From early times, they tried to stop these storms. Long ago, Native American women played a kind of field hockey called shinny. They thought playing the game made their fields and crops safe from sandstorms.

Today, experts are trying to stop sandstorms. But how? In China, where there are many sandstorms, people want to plant trees to make forests. Trees and plants can help stop sandstorms. The trees and plants stop the wind from blowing the sand into a big column. They form a wind-breaker that helps keep the sand and soil from moving around.

But, trees take time to grow. Trees need water and rich soil. People who study and care for Earth have a dream. They want to find ways to grow trees in the dry soil of the desert. They will keep working on their dream.

Using Our Knowledge

When a sandstorm hits, it brings strong winds and blowing sand. But, with the knowledge we have today, we are in a better position to keep ourselves safe. And we can also use our knowledge to find ways to protect Earth from these fierce storms.

Vo•**cab**•u•lar•y

fossils (**fos**•uhlz)—part of a plant or animal that lived long ago and was protected in the soil

preserved (pri•**zurvd**)—took care of and kept safe

Context Clues

You can often figure out the meaning of an unfamiliar word by reading its definition in the passage. The clue to the meaning of the word is often given in the same sentence or in a nearby sentence. When you use these clues, you are using **context clues**.

For example, in "Sandstorms," you read the following passage:

> *Weather stations, called satellites, are launched into space. They fly around Earth with radar cameras. The cameras take pictures of storms.*

Here the author defined *weather stations* for you as *satellites*. Did you notice that the definition of weather stations, "called satellites" was surrounded by commas? That can sometimes be a hint.

Read the following sentences. Notice that each word in boldface is defined in the sentence.

1. **Tornadoes**, or violent whirlwinds, cover a smaller area than hurricanes.
2. The **fog**, which is misty air at ground level, prevented the cars from traveling on the highway.
3. To **predict**—or foresee—the weather, the scientist must consider many things.

Read the following sentences. Each sentence has a boldface word that is defined within the sentence. On your own piece of paper, write the definition for the boldface word that is found within the sentence.

1. The **eye** of the storm, or its center, contains warm air.
2. **Cumulonimbus**, or storm clouds, gathered in the sky.
3. High **humidity**, or dampness in the air, makes people uncomfortable.
4. Air is easily **compressed**, or pressed together.
5. The **composition**, or makeup, of the air is much the same.

Diary Entry

You have finished reading an article about sandstorms. In a small group, practice reading this diary entry by a girl named Carla who experienced a sandstorm. Rehearse using good phrasing and expression. Then, read it aloud to your classmates.

Fluency

▶ TIP

Carla is writing about something exciting that happened in her life. Try to make your voice capture the excitement Carla felt as she experienced the sandstorm.

Dear Diary,

This week's big event was the sandstorm!

On Sunday, Mom and I took a walk. The weather was nice when we started, but then the wind really started to blow. We could hear it whistling through the trees. The wind kept getting stronger and stronger. Mom made us turn back. By the time we got home, the wind was blowing hard! It blew sand in my face. It stung. I could barely see!

We were so happy to get home. Dad turned on the TV news so we could hear the weather report. The reporter said a sandstorm was on its way. She said the wind might gust to 60 miles an hour. People were advised to stay inside and to bring in their pets.

When Dad heard this, he jumped out of his chair. Sparky was still in his doghouse! Dad ran outside to get Sparky. They were both covered with sand when they got back inside.

I was so happy when we were all inside and safe. We had to stay in our house for two days. We watched the weather reports and listened to the wind howl around the house. The meteorologist said the different temperatures of the sun and Earth were making the wind blow hard. I was a little scared. But now I'm thinking about someday becoming a meteorologist. Then I can help predict storms and tell people about how to stay safe. Still, I hope I'm never in a sandstorm again!

Steps in a Process

TO: Our Neighbors

FROM: Weather Service

RE: Hurricane on Its Way

A hurricane is making its way to our area. It will arrive in about 24 hours. You should protect your family and pets. You also need to protect your property. Here is what to do to keep safe:

If You Must Go:

1. Follow the instructions from your local weather service.

2. Follow your family plan.

3. Take your disaster supply kit.

4. Head to a shelter or other safe place.

If You Can Stay:

1. Nail boards over your windows.

2. Bring inside things that may fly in high winds, such as flowerpots and benches.

3. Keep your pets safe by bringing them inside.

4. Keep a kit of things to use in an emergency. Examples are a flashlight with fresh batteries and lots of water to drink.

Discussion Questions

Answer these questions with a partner or on a separate piece of paper.

1. Which of these is the last thing that should happen if you must evacuate before a hurricane?

   a. return to your home
   b. go to emergency shelter
   c. nail boards over your windows
   d. find a safe place for your pet

2. What should you have to make sure your flashlight works?

3. Why should your family have a hurricane or disaster plan?

4. Why should you put boards over the windows before the storm?

   a. Boards do not cost much money.
   b. You don't want to see out.
   c. You don't want neighbors to see in.
   d. Boards help prevent windows from breaking.

5. Besides people and property, what else in your house should you protect in a storm?

   a. your television
   b. your pets
   c. your front yard
   d. your snacks

6. What is the worst thing that may happen if flowerpots are left outside in a hurricane?

   a. They may hurt people as they fly.
   b. They may be stolen by others.
   c. The flowers may grow wild.
   d. They may land on a neighbor's bench.

7. What two things go in an emergency kit?

8. What is the purpose of the notice to "Our Neighbors" from the "Weather Service?"

CONNECTING
to the Real World

EXPLORE MORE

Perform a Skit
Imagine that a family of four is in their house before a hurricane or sandstorm. Write a script. Have the family members talk about what they will do to prepare for the storm.

Demonstrate a Sandstorm Scarf
Using a long scarf, demonstrate for the class how to protect your face during a sandstorm. Explain which parts of your face need to be protected and why.

Write a Report
Do research about a bad hurricane in the history of the United States. (An example is Hurricane Andrew.) Deliver your report to a small group or the whole class.

Make a Poster
Create a poster of safety tips on how to stay safe in a lightning storm. Draw a picture for the poster. Hang it in the classroom.

Write a Poem
With a classmate, write a poem about a hurricane, lightning, or a sandstorm. Illustrate your poem.

Create a Radio Broadcast
Imagine you are a weather forecaster. Deliver a weather broadcast that a sandstorm is coming. Tell people how to prepare.

Related Books

Berger, Melvin, and Gilda Berger. *Do Tornadoes Really Twist? Questions and Answers About Tornadoes and Hurricanes.* Scholastic, 2000.

Cole, Joanna, and Bruce Degen. *The Magic School Bus Inside a Hurricane.* Scholastic, 1996.

Gibbons, Gail. *Weather Words and What They Mean.* Holiday House, Inc., 1996.

Perry, Kate, and Jo Moore. *People Chase Twisters: And Other Amazing Facts About Violent Weather.* Millbrook Press, 1998.

Simon, Seymour. *Lightning.* William Morrow & Company, 1999.

—*Weather.* Harper Collins, 2000.

Interesting Web Sites

Hurricanes

www.nws.noaa.gov/om/reachout/kidspage.shtml

www.bwca.cc/weather/weatherblueprints.htm

www.miamisci.org/hurricane/rainmeasure/html

www.fema.gov/kids/hurr.htm

www.enchantedlearning.com/classroom/lookitup/weather.shtml

Lightning

www.energyquest.ca.gov/projects/lightning.html

Sandstorms

www.pbs.org/lawrenceofarabia/revolt/transport.html

Web sites have been carefully researched for accuracy, content, and appropriateness. However, teachers and caregivers are reminded that Web sites are subject to change. Internet use should always be monitored.

BEFORE READING

Set a Purpose

by skimming the selection to decide what I want to know about this subject.

DURING READING

Clarify Understanding

by deciding whether the information I'm reading is fact or opinion.

AFTER READING

Respond

by forming my own opinion about what I've read.

LEARN
the strategies
in the selection
Lance Armstrong
page 191

PRACTICE
the *strategies*
in the selection
Jackie Joyner-Kersee
page 203

APPLY
the *strategies*
in the selection
Jim Abbott
page 213

Think About
the
Strategies

BEFORE READING

Set a Purpose
by skimming the selection to decide what I want to know about this subject.

My Thinking
The strategy says to skim the selection to decide what I want to know about this subject. In looking quickly through the article's headings and text, I see that this selection is about Lance Armstrong and his bicycle races. I want to know who Lance Armstrong is and what he did to become famous. Now I'll read on.

DURING READING

Clarify Understanding
by deciding whether the information I'm reading is fact or opinion.

My Thinking
The strategy says to decide whether the information I'm reading is fact or opinion. I will stop and think about this strategy every time I come to a red button like this .

Lance Armstrong

Lance Armstrong handles a steep trail during the 2003 Tour de France.

What is the hardest sports event in the world? Many people say it is the Tour de France. They call it the "Super Bowl" of cycling. The Tour de France always starts and finishes in France. Riders pedal more than 2,000 miles. They face bumpy roads and steep mountains. The race lasts 3 weeks. Millions of fans come to watch, rain or shine.

Lance Armstrong won this race five times. And he won them all after a tough battle with **cancer**.

Lance wrote two books about his life. They show that he worked hard to reach the top. As for cancer, Lance calls it "a special wake-up call." He learned new lessons about life. Each day became a gift.

Vo•cab•u•lar•y

cancer (kan•suhr)—a disease in which sick cells grow in parts of the body where they do not belong

Growing Up

Lance was born on September 18, 1971. His mother, Linda, was only 17. She and his father were not married very long. Lance never met his father.

His first home was a tiny apartment in Dallas, Texas. Linda held 2 jobs while she went to school. Lance says she was a great mother. Each night, she read to him. She told him to follow his dreams and never give up.

Lance says his mother is his biggest hero.

At age 7, Lance got a cheap brown bicycle with yellow wheels. He loved to ride it.

By then, he was living in Plano, Texas. Football was the big sport there. Lance could run fast, but he did poorly in ball games. He wanted to succeed at sports. Lance worked hard at swimming. He became one of the best young swimmers in his state. Each day, he biked 20 miles to practice swimming at his school.

At age 13, Lance entered a junior **triathlon**. This race has three parts: biking, swimming, and running. His mother bought him a racing bike. Lance won! He went on to become the best junior triathlete in Texas.

Road to Fame

Lance enjoyed cycling most of all. He won some big **amateur** races. Soon, U.S. Olympic coaches asked him to train with other gifted cyclists.

In 1992, Lance entered his first professional cycling race. It was held in Spain. Lance lost. In fact, he came in *last* place. ●

So, Lance worked harder. He trained for hours each day in all kinds of weather. When he fell, he got back on. He rode even when he was tired or sore.

His efforts paid off. Lance won ten races in 1993. Now he was a world-class cyclist. Fans cheered for him.

For eight months each year, Lance raced in Europe. Often, he was the only American racing. Few Americans had won the top races. He was making history.

> ## Strategy
>
> **Clarify Understanding** by deciding whether the information I'm reading is fact or opinion.
>
> My Thinking
> The story says that at age 13, Lance won a junior triathlon. This must be fact because I can check racing records to see if that's so. I can also check to see how Lance did in Spain in 1992.

Lance was determined to succeed.

> ## Vo·**cab**·u·lar·y
>
> **triathlon** (try•**ath**•luhn)— a race in which people must run, ride a bicycle, and swim certain distances
>
> **amateur** (**am**•uh•tur)— unpaid; not professional

Strategy

Clarify Understanding by deciding whether the information I'm reading is fact or opinion.

My Thinking
The story says that the doctors told Lance he had cancer. This must be fact because I can check that in newspaper articles or in Lance's book.

Shocking News

In 1996, Lance turned 25. He was winning major titles. In Texas, he owned a big new house with a pool. He was becoming successful.

That spring, he was the first American to win a tough mountain race in France. Then, Lance **placed** second in a 1-day race that was 167 miles long. In North Carolina, he won another big mountain race.

But something was wrong. He felt bad pains when he sat on his bike. A doctor checked Lance and did some tests.

The news was grim: Lance had cancer. Doctors said he had less than a 40 percent chance to live. Lance wrote about his fears: "I'll never be able to race again." "I'll die." "I'll never have a family."

Doctors performed surgery the next day. They took out some of the cancer. The cancer had spread to more areas of his body. Lance needed brain surgery, too. More cancer was in his lungs. Lance took special anticancer drugs. They made him feel sicker. He lost weight. But he was glad to be alive.

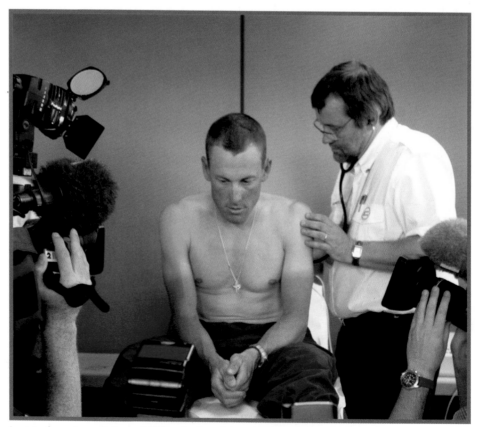

Lance became sick and thin during his cancer treatments.

Vo·cab·u·lar·y

placed (playst)—ranked in a series or group

[194]

Back on Top

Friends and family helped Lance during his illness. He started helping other people with cancer, too. He formed the Lance Armstrong Foundation to help raise money and **awareness**.

Slowly, Lance started riding his bike again. But would he ever **compete** again?

Lance was unsure. In 1998, he began training harder. He entered some races. People were surprised when he won or did well.

The 1999 Tour de France began. Could Lance possibly win? Fans cheered when he was the first to cross the finish line. Reporters called it the biggest sports comeback ever.

But Lance reminded others of something even more important. He was the first cancer **survivor** to win. That gave people hope.

Lance raced in the 2000 Summer Olympics. He won the Tour de France that year, as well.

Then he won the 2001 Tour de France. In 2002, he won again. He was the first and only American to win four times. Only four other men had won this race four times.

Could Lance win five in a row? Fans were thrilled when he did just that in 2003. Only one other man had won five in a row. He is Miguel Indurain of Spain. Lance told reporters he would not retire. He hoped to win more races.

Strategy

Clarify Understanding by deciding whether the information I'm reading is fact or opinion.

My Thinking
The story says that Lance won the Tour de France in 2000. This must be fact because the racing records confirm it.

Top Winners in the Tour de France	
Lance Armstrong (U.S.)	1999, 2000, 2001, 2002, 2003
Miguel Indurain (Spain)	1991, 1992, 1993, 1994, 1995
Bernard Hinault (France)	1978, 1979; 1981, 1982; 1985
Eddie Merckx (Belgium)	1969, 1970, 1971, 1972
Jacques Anquetil (France)	1957; 1961, 1962, 1963, 1964

Vo·cab·u·lar·y

awareness (uh•**wair**•nuhs)— knowledge, information

compete (kuhm•**peet**)— to take part in a contest or race

survivor (suhr•**vy**•vuhr)— one who lives through a deadly event

My Thinking
I think the information about Lance Armstrong being a hero is an opinion. I think he is a hero, but it is not something I can check or look up in a book. That is just how I feel. That is how the author of this article feels, too.

A Sports Legend

No matter how many more times he wins, Lance will always be a sports legend. To many people, he is a hero. One sportswriter wrote, "He's become a kind of hope machine."

The Lance Armstrong Foundation helps people with cancer in many ways. It raises money for **research**. It also helps people learn more about the disease.

Lance helped raise awareness and money for cancer patients.
INSET: Fellow racer Eddie Merckx (above right) calls Lance "a great racer and a great person."

Vo·cab·u·lar·y

research (rih•**surch**)—to study something in a careful way

Lance Armstrong is a winner in many ways. Not only has he won many races, but he has triumphed over personal challenges, as well.

Hard work and courage made Lance Armstrong a winner. His story inspires people around the world.

Think About the Strategy

AFTER READING

Respond
by forming my own opinion about what I've read.

My Thinking

The strategy says to form my own opinion about what I've read. That means I must decide how I feel about it. My opinion is that Lance Armstrong is strong and brave. He is a great racer because he has won so many Tour de France races. He is brave because he battled cancer and defeated that, too.

Graphic organizers help us organize information. An order chain organizes events in a time order. It shows how one step follows another step. To get started, you ask, "What happened or was done first?" Then you need to figure out the other steps. Finally, you identify the last, or final, step. Here is how I organized my order chain.

Order Chain
Lance Armstrong

First Step—Armstrong was born on September 18, 1971, in Dallas, Texas.

↓

Next Step—At age 7, he loved to ride his bicycle. He also loved swimming. Each day he biked 20 miles to practice swimming.

↓

Next Step—At age 13, he won a junior triathlon race. It had biking, swimming, and running.

↓

Next Step—In 1992, he entered his first professional cycling race. He came in last. So, he worked harder at his sport.

↓

Next Step—In 1993, he won 10 races. He was now a world-class cyclist.

↓

Next Step—At 21, he became a world champ at a race in Norway.

↓

Next Step—In 1996, he turned 25. His doctors told him he had cancer. It was serious. He had treatments.

↓

Next Step—Armstrong got better. He competed again. He won many races. By 2003, he had won 5 Tour de France races in a row.

↓

Final Step—Today, Armstrong is a sports legend. He is also the first cancer survivor to win the big race.

I used my graphic organizer to write a summary of Lance Armstrong's life. Can you find the information in my summary that came from my order chain?

A Summary of
Lance Armstrong

One of the hardest sports events is a bicycle race called the Tour de France. Cyclists ride 2,000 miles over difficult roads. Lance Armstrong won the Tour de France 5 years in a row. That alone is a feat. Lance won the Tour de France after he recovered from cancer.

Lance was born on September 18, 1971, in Dallas, Texas. His mother, Linda, was very young. Linda raised Lance by herself. Her strength and hard work inspired him during his life. When he was 7, he liked to swim and ride his bicycle. Each day he biked 20 miles to swim at his school. When he was 13, he won a junior triathlon race. It combined biking, swimming, and running in 1 event. Later he became the best junior triathlete in Texas.

Lance liked cycling the most out of all three sports. He entered his first professional cycling race in 1992. He came in last but he did not give up. Instead, he worked harder at the sport. In 1993, he won 10 races, making him a world-class cyclist. Lance was one of only a few Americans to win world-class races.

In 1996, he turned 25. One day Lance felt pain while cycling. When he went to the doctor, he had a few tests. The doctor found that Lance had cancer. It was so serious that Lance had surgery the next day. After the surgery, the cancer continued to spread. Lance needed more surgery and medicine to try to stop it. Lance got better with help from friends and family. As he felt better, he raised money and awareness for the disease.

Lance started to train again just 2 years later. He competed in the 1999 Tour de France and won. In 2000, Lance competed in the summer Olympics and won the Tour de France. His winning streak continued. By 2003, he had won the Tour de France 5 years in a row. Miguel Indurain is the only other person to win 5 years in a row. Lance is the first cancer survivor to win the Tour de France. He is a sports legend.

Lance Armstrong's courage and hard work has helped him in many ways. He inspires many people. Lance is a great athlete and a cancer survivor.

Introduction
Here is my introduction. It tells what I will write about.

Body
I used information from my order chain for my body paragraphs. The first paragraph comes from the "First Step." The following paragraphs come from the information in the "Next Steps." The "Final Step" on the order chain is the last paragraph in my body.

Conclusion
I concluded my paper by summarizing some of the main ideas.

Idioms

An **idiom** is a phrase with a special meaning. The meaning of the idiom is more than the meanings of the words in the phrase. For example, you probably know the idiom *I could eat a horse!* This idiom means the speaker is very hungry, but he won't really eat a horse! *He threw in the towel* is another idiom. This idiom means that someone has given up on something. This idiom came from the sport of boxing. If a fighter wanted to quit, he really would throw in his towel. People use idioms when they talk all the time.

The following sentence from "Lance Armstrong" has an idiom.

> *To many people, he is a hero. One sportswriter wrote, "He's become a kind of hope machine."*

The idiom in the passage above is "a hope machine." You can tell it is an idiom because Lance Armstrong is not really a hope machine.

Read each of the following sentences. Each sentence contains an idiom in boldface. Number your own sheet of paper from 1 to 5. Then, look at the list of meanings following the sentences. Choose the meaning that matches the idiom and write the letter after the correct number.

1. The teacher used a game **to break the ice** with her new class.
2. Syd had **ants in his pants** at the start of the race.
3. The storm was coming fast and it was **raining cats and dogs**.
4. Shane had **to work like a dog** to get the team ready for the big race.
5. Celine **counted her chickens before they hatched** when she celebrated winning before the game was over.

a. to work hard

b. someone who is restless

c. to expect to get something before you really do

d. to help people relax

e. raining hard

Television Report

Read the following television report to yourself. Imagine that you are the reporter describing the end of the 2003 Tour de France. When you are ready, read it aloud to the class.

Fluency TIP

The TV audience should hear the excitement in your voice as sports great Lance Armstrong reaches the finish line.

Will It Be Five Tours for Lance?

How does Lance do this? He has had cancer, and he is in his 30s! But here he is, about to win his 5th Tour de France in a row!

Some people call this the most demanding sports event in the world. It has not been an easy Tour for Lance. He has had to work harder than he did in the past 4 Tours. But each time something goes wrong, Lance gets up again. He knows how to compete. He is a great athlete. Even when he was an amateur competing in local triathlons, Lance never gave up.

Lance and the other lead cyclists in the Tour de France are now riding up to the finish line in Paris. Thousands of fans crowd the street. Lance wears the yellow jersey with pride. He and the other cyclists deserve all the applause. They have been riding their bikes for 3 weeks. They have ridden more than 2,000 miles! That is an awful lot of land to cover, even if you are in a car. But Lance and the other cyclists did this all on their own. It's pedal power!

Lance's muscles must be aching. But this man is a survivor. He has worked hard for this moment. He smiles and waves to the crowd. He savors the moment of this great success.

Bravo, Lance Armstrong!

Think About
the
Strategies

BEFORE READING

Set a Purpose
by skimming the selection to decide what I want to know about this subject.

 Write notes on your own paper to tell how you used this strategy.

DURING READING

Clarify Understanding
by deciding whether the information I'm reading is fact or opinion.

When you come to a red button like this ⬤, write notes on your own paper to tell how you used this strategy.

JACKIE JOYNER-KERSEE

A Big Day

It was a big day. It was the 1984 Olympic Games. Jackie Joyner-Kersee and her brother, Al Joyner, had both won medals. Jackie came in second place in the **heptathlon**. She won a silver medal. Al came in first place in the triple jump. The triple jump is a jump for distance made by hopping, striding, and jumping. He won a gold medal.

In the Olympics, athletes receive medals for winning. They win gold medals for first place. They win silver medals for second place. They win bronze medals for third place.

Jackie was happy for Al. She was proud that he won a gold medal. She knew that Al had worked hard to win. The years of his love for track had paid off. He had done his best. He worked hard and won the gold medal.

Vo • **cab** • u • lar • y

heptathlon
(hep•**tath**•luhn)— a sporting contest with seven track and field events

[203]

Strategy

Clarify Understanding
by deciding whether the
information I'm reading is
fact or opinion.

Write notes on your
own paper to tell how
you used this strategy.

Jackie practices the high jump.

Jackie was not as happy with herself. She came in second place. She was thankful to win a silver medal. But she knew that she could do better.

Heptathlon athletes run the 100-meter **hurdles** and the 200-meter dash. They also complete the 800-meter run. They throw the shot, called shot put, and the **javelin**. They do the high jump and the long jump.

Jackie knew she could run faster with more **practice**. She knew she could jump and throw farther. Jackie knew she could win a gold medal.

Jackie practices the long jump.

Vo•**cab**•u•lar•y

hurdles (**hur**•dlz)—objects that runners must leap over in a race

javelin (**jav**•lin)—a light spear thrown for distance

practice (**prak**•tis)— the act of doing something over and over in order to get better

Going to Make It

Jackie's full name is Jacqueline Joyner-Kersee. Her grandmother named her after the wife of President John F. Kennedy. The wife of the president is called the First Lady. When Jackie was born, her grandmother said, "Someday this girl will be the First Lady of something."

The Joyners lived in East St. Louis, Illinois. Mr. Joyner was a construction worker. He also worked on the railroad. Mrs. Joyner was a nurse's **aide**. Mr. and Mrs. Joyner worked hard. But the family was poor. At times they did not have enough food to eat.

The Joyners lived in a small house. The house was in an unsafe part of town. As a child, Jackie saw a man get shot on her street. Their mother kept Jackie and Al from such danger. She taught them to study hard. She taught them to be kind to others. Jackie and Al knew that their parents worked hard. But they wanted a better life. They made a promise that one day they were going to "make it."

A Rising Star

Jackie and Al spent much of their free time at a community center. Here they could learn, exercise, and play sports. They stayed away from the dangers of the streets. At first, Jackie took dance lessons at the center. Al joined the swim team. In time, Jackie and Al joined the track and field team. Track and field became their love.

> **Strategy**
>
> **Clarify Understanding** by deciding whether the information I'm reading is fact or opinion.
>
> Write notes on your own paper to tell how you used this strategy.

Jackie with brother Al

Vo·cab·u·lar·y

aide (ayd)—a helper

[205]

Strategy

Clarify Understanding by deciding whether the information I'm reading is fact or opinion.

Write notes on your own paper to tell how you used this strategy.

Jackie and Al grew close. They helped each other become better athletes. They liked to compete against each other. One time, Al challenged Jackie to a race down the street. He said he could beat her without practice. Not only was Al a boy, but he was two years older. Still, Jackie agreed to a race. The challenge made her want to work harder.

Jackie practiced every day before the race. As promised, Al did not practice at all. When the day of the race came, Jackie was ready. Many kids from the neighborhood came to watch. Jackie and Al raced from the corner of the street to the front of their house. Jackie's hard work paid off. She won the race!

Jackie practiced and practiced. She worked hard at the track and field events. In high school, she became a state **champion**. Jackie also did well in school. She studied and got good grades. She was able to go to college. There she joined the track and field team.

Hurdles in Life

Jackie went to college at UCLA—a long way from home. It was hard for Jackie to be so far from home. At the end of the first school year, something **tragic** happened. Jackie's mother suddenly died from a **rare** illness.

With the help of her brother Al, Jackie stayed strong. She did not let the sadness slow her down. The death of her mother made her want to **succeed** even more. Jackie's coach, Bob Kersee, also helped her. Bob took her under his wing and helped her get through this hard time. He was Jackie's friend and her coach. Later, they married.

Jackie completes her long jump.

Vo•cab•u•lar•y

champion (**cham**•pee•uhn)— a person who wins first place in a contest

tragic (**traj**•ik)—unfortunate, disastrous

rare—not occurring often

succeed (suhk•**seed**)—to do what you set out to do

Jackie faced another personal challenge. In college, Jackie learned that she had a condition called **asthma**. Asthma makes air tubes in the lungs **shrink**. Asthma made it hard for her to breathe when she ran. At first, she believed that she was out of shape. She thought she was not working hard enough. She didn't know that she had asthma.

Having asthma made Jackie want to work harder. She saw asthma as an **opponent** that she had to defeat. She listened to what her doctor told her to do. She took her medicine. She kept working hard. She did not let asthma keep her from her dream.

Heptathlon Events

Event	Description
100-meter hurdles	Athletes race for 100 meters (about 330 feet) while leaping over hurdles.
high jump	Athletes jump over a bar that is raised above the ground. The athlete who jumps over the highest bar wins.
shot put	Athletes compete to see who can throw a heavy metal ball the farthest.
200-meter dash	Athletes race for 200 meters (about 660 feet).
long jump	Athletes compete to see who can jump the farthest with a running start.
javelin throw	Athletes compete to see who can throw a javelin the farthest.
800-meter run	Athletes race for 800 meters (about 2,600 feet).

Vo•cab•u•lar•y

asthma (**az**•muh)—a disease that makes it difficult to breathe

shrink (**shringk**)—to become smaller

opponent (uh•**poh**•nuhnt)—a person or force that one competes against

Jackie achieved her dream.

Olympic Success

After Jackie won the silver medal in 1984, she continued to practice. The more she practiced, the better she became. On July 7, 1986, she set the world record. In the next two years, she broke her own world record two more times.

At the 1988 Olympic Games in Seoul, Korea, Jackie was given a second chance to win the gold medal. The 1988 Olympics was the high point of her career. She won a gold medal in the long jump. She also won a gold medal in the heptathlon. She set the world record in both events.

In the 1992 Olympics in Spain, she won her third and final gold medal.

Living Her Dream

Jackie lived out her dream. With practice and much hard work, she "made it." She made it to the Olympics. She won three gold medals, one silver, and one bronze. Most importantly, she **achieved** her personal best. She overcame personal hurdles. Having a medical condition that affected her breathing did not stop her. She listened to her doctors, her coach, and her own body. She did not let it defeat her.

Vo•cab•u•lar•y

achieved (uh•**cheevd**)—
reached by effort

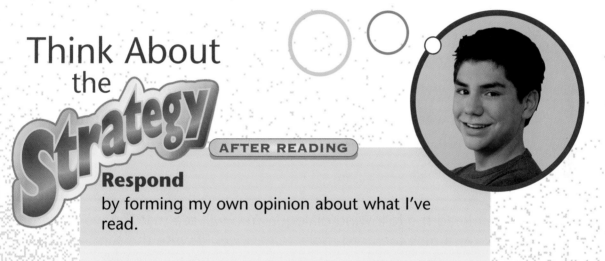

Think About the Strategy

AFTER READING

Respond
by forming my own opinion about what I've read.

 Write notes on your own paper to tell how you used this strategy.

Synonyms

A **synonym** is a word that has the same meaning—or almost the same meaning—as another word. Sometimes when you read, it is helpful to think of synonyms for words you are reading. That helps you learn new words. Sometimes when you write, you can make your story more interesting if you use a synonym for a word you have used many times.

In "Jackie Joyner-Kersee," you read this sentence:

> *The house was in an **unsafe** part of town.*

If you were to think of synonyms for *unsafe*, you might come up with *dangerous* or *risky*.

You also read this sentence in "Jackie Joyner-Kersee."

> *In high school, she became a state **champion**.*

If you were to think of synonyms for *champion*, you might come up with *winner* or *victor*.

Read the following dialogue. You will see that the words **said** and **nice** are used more than once. Rewrite the sentences. Choose a synonym from the list to replace the boldface word. After you have finished, reread the dialogue. Think about how the new words (synonyms) make the dialogue more interesting.

replied	decent	declared
fantastic	concluded	stated

1. "I'm looking forward to our track meet on Saturday," Francis **said** to Dan.

2. "Yes, me too," **said** Dan.

3. "The weather is supposed to be **nice**."

4. "I hope so," **said** Dan, "the rain last week was awful."

5. "It would also be **nice** if we won this week," said Francis.

6. "Either way," **said** Dan, "we'll still have fun!"

Radio Report

Read this radio report to yourself. Imagine that you are a reporter delivering a report on sports great Jackie Joyner-Kersee in 1992. When you are ready, read the report aloud to the class. You may want to use an imaginary microphone.

Fluency ▶ **TIP**

Try to make the speed of your reading reflect the excitement of your report. Decide what you think are the exciting parts of the report. Read those parts with more excitement. The less exciting parts should be read in a slower and more informative voice.

The First Lady of Track and Field

This is an up-close and personal report on Jackie Joyner-Kersee by your sports reporter.

Jackie Joyner-Kersee, the track and field athlete, won two gold medals at the 1988 Olympic Games. She won in the long jump. She also got the gold in the heptathlon event.

Today, here at the 1992 Olympic Games in Spain, Jackie won another gold medal! That's not easy to do in the grueling heptathlon event! Jackie knows how to succeed. She knows how to achieve her goals. How does she do it? Practice, practice, practice!

She throws the javelin and jumps the hurdles over and over again. She practices the triple jump until her legs give out. She runs endless laps around the track. And when she competes in a sports event, she gives it her all.

Jackie has asthma. It isn't always easy for her to breathe. But this proud champion will not let this disease beat her. Jackie has heart. She has earned our respect. She is the First Lady of track and field!

Think About the

Strategies

BEFORE READING

Set a Purpose

by skimming the selection to decide what I want to know about this subject.

DURING READING

Clarify Understanding

by deciding whether the information I'm reading is fact or opinion.

AFTER READING

Respond

by forming my own opinion about what I've read.

 Use your own paper to jot notes to apply these Before, During, and After Reading Strategies. In this selection, you will choose when to stop, think, and respond.

JIM ABBOTT

Jim in action on the pitching mound

Jim Abbott always wanted to **pitch**. He played in Little League and college. He pitched in the Olympics. And he pitched for some of the best teams in the major leagues—the top level of professional baseball teams. Jim Abbott was a great baseball pitcher.

It is not easy to have a **career** as an athlete. You must have a special **talent** in your sport. Jim had that. But he was even more unique. He played with only one hand.

A Love for Sports

Jim was born in Flint, Michigan, in 1967. His parents were happy to welcome their new baby. Jim was the young couple's first child. His brother, Chad, was born a few years later.

Vo • cab • u • lar • y

pitch (pich)—to throw a baseball toward a batter in a baseball game

career (kuh•reer)—the kind of work a person does to make a living

talent (tal•uhnt)—the ability to do something well

When he was born, Jim did not have a right hand. His right arm ended in a flap of skin. It is hard to do many things with only one hand. But having one hand was all he had ever known. It felt perfectly natural to him. As time would prove, having only one hand would not be a real **disability** to Jim. For him, it was just an extra challenge.

Jim loved sports. But his parents did not know what to do. Should they **encourage** his interest? They wanted to protect him from being made fun of by other kids. Those kids might say ugly things to Jim about having only one hand.

They tried to interest Jim in soccer, because soccer is played mostly with the legs and feet. That might be easier for a boy with one hand. But Jim wanted to follow his own path. Of all sports, he liked baseball best.

To play baseball, you must be able to run fast. You need to be able to hit the ball with a bat. You also need to field balls. This means you have to be able to catch and throw. And some people, like Jim, like to pitch.

How could Jim do all these things with only one hand?

Baseball His Own Way

The young Jim found his own way to pitch *and* field balls. To pitch, he put a baseball glove over the end of his right arm. After making his pitch, he quickly slid his left hand into the glove. This let him catch any balls that were batted his way.

How would he throw after catching a ball? After making a catch, Jim cradled the glove on his right arm and slipped his left hand out of the glove. He then grabbed the ball with his left hand and threw it. He did all these things fast. He practiced and practiced until he got it just right.

As he started in Little League, Jim showed everyone that he could play well with one hand. Batters would test him. They would **bunt** the ball. But to Jim, these were easy outs. He ran and quickly scooped up the ball. He then tapped the runner out himself or threw the ball to first base.

Vo·cab·u·lar·y

disability (dis•uh•**bil**•i•tee)—a special physical or mental challenge

encourage (en•**kur**•ij)— to urge or inspire; help to make something happen

bunt—a baseball play in which the batter hits the ball so it lands close to home plate

Early Fame—in Football!

Everyone in Jim's hometown knew about the one-handed Little Leaguer. But it was through football that he would become known around the whole country.

By high school, Jim was a good all-around athlete. He could play many sports well. He was tall and strong. At Flint Central High School, Jim was named the quarterback for the school team. This is an important position in football.

At one game, a reporter noticed Jim. He wrote about how well this one-handed quarterback played. Many newspapers picked up the article. Lots of people read about Jim.

College Baseball—and the Olympics!

Jim could have become a professional athlete right out of high school. However, he was also an honors student. Education was important to him. He decided to go to college first.

But that did not mean he had to give up sports. At the University of Michigan, he won a spot on the baseball team. He did a good job as pitcher. Even more people heard about him.

Jim pitched for various major league teams.

After a couple of years, Jim decided to join Team USA. They traveled around the world. They played against teams from other countries.

In 1988, Jim played on the U.S. Olympic baseball team in Seoul, South Korea. He turned 21 years old that week. And he helped lead the team to the gold medal!

Life in the Major Leagues

The next year, Jim turned professional. He went to pitch for the California Angels. The Angels are a major league baseball team. Most players first go to minor league teams—the lower levels of professional baseball teams.

Some people thought the Angels hired Jim because he was famous. They did not think a one-handed player could do well in the major leagues. Jim proved them wrong. He won the respect of other players. He worked hard. He was also kind and pleasant. He did not let the attention go to his head.

One dream of every pitcher is to pitch a no-hitter game—a baseball game in which no batter can make a hit. A pitcher does not like to hear that big *crack* when a bat connects well with the ball. In 1993, pitching for the New York Yankees, Jim pitched a no-hitter against the Cleveland Indians. It was a **satisfying** day.

Jim pitched for various major league teams for 10 years. Some years, his pitching was great. Other years, he struggled. Jim did not always do well. But he always gave it his best.

Jim had a ten-year career in the major leagues.

Vo•cab•u•lar•y

satisfying (sat•is•fy•ing)— fulfilling; gratifying

[216]

Moving On

In 1999, Jim retired from baseball. It was time to move on to other things. He said, "My career wasn't always great, but it was wonderful."

Today Jim speaks to groups about doing their best. He tells people that it is what you *do* with your life, not what you *cannot* do, that counts.

Jim Abbott has made his mark on the world through his professional and personal strengths. He is a man to be admired.

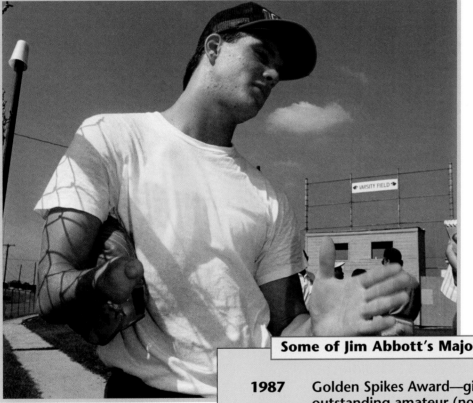

Today Jim talks to people about how to succeed in life.

Some of Jim Abbott's Major Awards and Honors

1987	Golden Spikes Award—given to the nation's outstanding amateur (nonprofessional) baseball player
1987	Sports Award for Courage
1988	March of Dimes Amateur Athlete of the Year Award
1988	Tanqueray Achievement Award—given to outstanding amateur athletes
1988	Sullivan Award—the United States' highest honor for an amateur athlete
1988	U.S. Olympics Baseball Team Gold Medal—pitcher
1990	American League Cy Young Award—third place in voting

Context Clues

You can often figure out the meaning of a word by looking for a **context clue**. Context clues are other words or ideas that are related to the unfamiliar word. Context clues give clues to the meaning of the word you don't know.

In "Jim Abbott," you read this passage:

> *In 1999, Jim retired from baseball. It was time to move on to other things.*

The words *move on to other things* give a clue that *retired* means "to leave what you are doing."

Read the following sentences. Look at the word or words in bold-face. These words are context clues to help explain the unfamilar word in italics.

1. The fox *struggled* with the snake until he **fought off** the attacker.
2. The doctor *operated* on the patient by **making a cut** in her heart and **repairing** a valve.
3. Janet *lingered* outside the school for a long time but got tired of **waiting**.

Read the following sentences. On a separate sheet of paper, write the words in the sentence that are clues to the meaning of the word in boldface.

1. We **hiked** in the woods and ended up walking ten miles.
2. Mrs. Jones **stirred** the soup by moving the spoon around inside the pot.
3. A word in my report was misspelled. I **corrected** it when I changed the *e* to an *i*.
4. Michael **juggled** the balls. He threw them up and caught them on their way down.
5. The kitten made beautiful music as she continued to purr her **melody**.

Letter

Read the following question-and-answer letter exchange between a student and a sports expert. The student asks about baseball legend Jim Abbott. Take turns reading the questions and answers aloud with expression.

Fluency ▶ TIP

As you practice the part of Mr. Sports, make your voice sound like that of a sports expert. As you practice the part of the student, make your voice sound interested and excited.

Dear Mr. Sports

Dear Mr. Sports:

How did Jim Abbott become a professional ball player? How could you do that with just one hand?

Sami

Dear Sami:

How did Jim do it? He did it through talent and hard work. He found a way to play well despite his disability. It was a challenge. But Jim did not let it run his life.

He learned how to move the baseball glove quickly between his arms. He put his baseball glove over the end of his right arm. After he pitched, he slid his left hand quickly into the glove. When he caught balls, he cradled the glove on his right arm and slipped his left hand out of the glove. He grabbed the ball with his left hand and then threw it. That way, he could pitch, then catch and throw the ball.

Jim worked hard. He practiced a lot. And he received lots of encouragement from his family and his hometown community in Flint, Michigan. He became so good that he went straight into the major leagues of professional baseball. He didn't have to spend time in the minor leagues, like most baseball players do. He had a fine career in sports.

Keep working out, Sami. Jim Abbott has shown us that effort and practice pay off!

Mr. Sports

Directions

Obstacle Course

You and your classmates can have fun completing an obstacle course.

Build the Course

In a gym or yard, put tape on the floor for Start. Place four things on the floor, about five feet apart:

- Large pillow
- Small pillow
- Large plastic ring
- Beanbag

Run the Course

Use a stopwatch to time each person as he or she finishes the course. Go one at a time. The person who finishes in the least amount of time wins.

1. Begin at Start. Run around the large pillow [A] two times.

2. Move on to the small pillow [B]. Face backwards. Run around once.

3. Move on to the large plastic ring [C]. Hop around once.

4. Move to the beanbag [D]. Keeping one hand on the bag, take baby steps around twice.

5. Run back to the starting position.

On a separate piece of paper, keep track of your time on the course. Then try the course a second time. See if you can improve your time.

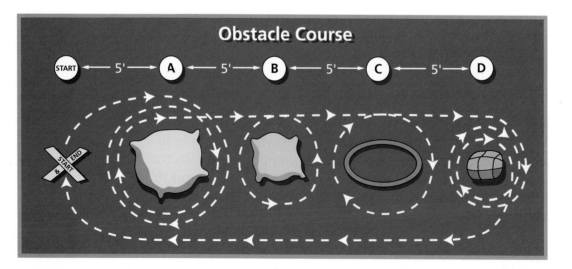

Discussion Questions

Answer these questions with a partner or on a separate sheet of paper.

1. At the start of the race, which of these will the runner reach first?

   a. beanbag
   b. large plastic ring
   c. small pillow
   d. large pillow

2. Around which thing does the runner face backwards?

   a. small pillow
   b. large pillow
   c. beanbag
   d. large plastic ring

3. About how many feet in all will the runner go in the full race?

   a. more than 40 feet
   b. 20 feet
   c. more than a mile
   d. less than 10 feet

4. In the race, the word *obstacle* means:

   a. large or flat.
   b. dance.
   c. something soft.
   d. something in the way.

5. In the second try of the obstacle course, how might a runner cut time from the first try?

6. Which is the only obstacle that a racer touches with his or her hand?

7. Why does it take less time to go from 4 to the end of the race than to go from Start to 4?

8. Why should the race be held in a large space?

CONNECTING
to the Real World

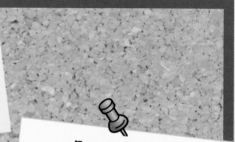

EXPLORE MORE

Make a Poster

Pick an athlete you like. Use crayons to make a poster of special things he or she has done. Hang your poster on a bulletin board.

Talk It Over

Pick a star athlete you like. Research the athlete. With a classmate, have a talk about how the star reached his or her goals.

Reach Success

Ask an adult for a goal he or she has reached in life. Find out what that person did to reach the goal. Start making a list of things to do to help you reach your goals.

Write a Report

Research another athlete who has had to overcome an obstacle to reach success. Write a report about him or her. Be sure to include pictures.

Sing Out!

Make up a song or poem about your favorite sports star. Write down the words. Sing or say a song or poem into a tape recorder. Play it for your classmates.

Make a Bookmark

Read a book about a person in sports who made a difference. Then make a bookmark about the person. List two special things he or she has done. Draw a picture of him or her. Share the book and the bookmark with your classmates.

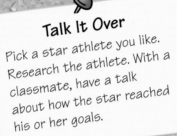

Related Books

Armstrong, Kristen. *Lance Armstrong: The Race of His Life.* Grosset and Dunlap, 2000.

Burby, Liza N. *Jackie Joyner-Kersee.* Rosen Publishing Group, 2001.

Christopher, Matt, and Glenn Stout. *On the Bike with . . . Lance Armstrong.* Little, Brown, 2003.

Goldstein, Margaret J. *Jackie Joyner-Kersee: Superwoman.* Lerner Publications Company, 1994.

Green, Carl. R. *Jackie Joyner-Kersee.* Crestwood House, 1994.

Harrington, Geri. *Jackie Joyner-Kersee: Champion Athlete.* Chelsea House Publisher, 1995.

Johnson, Rick L. *Beating the Odds.* Dillon Press, 1991.

Rambeck, Richard. *Jackie Joyner-Kersee.* The Child's World, 1997.

—*Jim Abbott.* The Child's World, 1994.

Reiser, Howard. *Jim Abbott: All-American Pitcher.* Children's Press, 1993.

Rolfe, John. *Jim Abbott.* Sports Illustrated for Kids, 1991.

Savage, Jeff. *Sports Great Jim Abbott.* Enslow Publishers, Inc. 1993.

Startt, James. *Tour de France/Tour de Force: A Visual History of the World's Greatest Bicycle Race.* Chronicle Books, 2000.

Stewart, Mark. *Sweet Victory: Lance Armstrong's Incredible Journey: The Amazing Story of the Greatest Comeback in Sports.* Millbrook Press, 2000.

Wilcockson, John. *The 2001 Tour de France: Lance x3.* VeloPress, 2001.

Interesting Web Sites

Check out the following Web sites for more information about the athletes in this unit.

www.sikids.com

Lance Armstrong
www.cyclingnews.com/road/2002/tour02/
www.espn.go.com/oly/tdf2003/index/html
www.lancearmstrong.com/
www.letour.fr/2003/us/live.html
www.roadcycling.com/events/tdf2003/

Jackie Joyner-Kersee
www.galegroup.com/free_resources/bhm/bio/joyner_j.htm
www.sacbee.com/static/archive/news/projects/people_of_century/sports/kersee.html

Jim Abbott
www.baseballlibrary.com/baseballlibrary/ballplayers/A/Abbott_Jim.stm
http://espn.go.com/mlb/profiles/profile/4308.html

Web sites have been carefully researched for accuracy, content, and appropriateness. However, teachers and caregivers are reminded that Web sites are subject to change. Internet use should always be monitored.